·EX· LIBRIS

Love Many Things

Kersty Evans

2016

About the Author

Kersty Evans is an artist, who has been writing stories since the age of seven, and drawing even earlier. Blessed with a vivid imagination, as well as a variety of life experiences, ideas never run out. Originally from the UK (London, Dorset, Cornwall) she has been living in Kilkenny since 2006.

Kersty left school aged 16 and has ever since been studying at the University of Life. She loves animals, enjoys art and design, fashion, freestyle disco dancing, gardening and of course, writing. She has an interest in history, mythology, travel and current affairs, likes music, books, films and theatre.

Love Many Things

Kersty Evans

Dun Emer Press
2016

Love Many Things.

Book; Short Stories.
2016

Published by.
Dun Emer Press.
2nd Flr, 13 Upr Baggot Street,
Dublin. D04 W7K5 Ireland.

Isbn No;.
978-0-9568202-6-6

Registered on Nielsen Book Data.

Printed by;

Eprint.35, Coolmine Industrial Estate, Dublin 15.

Dun Emer Press, is a registered Charity.
with 'The Charities Regulatory Authority'.

Front Cover painting by Kersty Evans

Book design Anthony Kelly

But I cannot help thinking that the best way of knowing God is to love many things.

Letter from Vincent van Gogh (1853-1890) to his brother Theo van Gogh(1857-1891), Cuesmes, Belgium, July 1880.

The Dun Emer Press
(1902–1908)

Dun Emer Press was an Irish private press founded in 1902 by
Elizabeth Yeats and her brother William Butler Yeats, part of the
Celtic Revival. It was named after the legendary Emer and evolved
into the Cuala Press.

In 1902, Elizabeth and her sister Lily Yeats joined Evelyn Gleeson
in establishing a craft studio at Dundrum, near Dublin, called Dun
Emer. This specialized in printing and other crafts, with Elizabeth
Yeats in charge of the printing press. While living in London,
Elizabeth Yeats had been part of the circle of William Morris,
and had been inspired by his printing work. Gleeson offered the
Yeats sisters her large house in Dundrum, in which a crafts group
providing training and work for young women, in the fields of
bookbinding, printing, weaving, and embroidery, could live and
work. Bookbinding workshops were a later addition to the studio.

The Dun Emer studio and press were named after Emer, daughter
of Forgall Monach, wife of the hero Cúchulainn in the Ulster Cycle
of Irish mythology, a figure famous for her artistic skills as well
as her beauty.The title-page device of the Dun Emer Press was
designed by Elinor Monsell and shows Emer standing underneath a
tree. Monsell also created the symbol of the Abbey Theatre, Dublin,
which depicts Maeve with a wolfhound. The focus of the Press was
on publishing literary work by Irish authors, and Elizabeth and Lily
Yeats's younger brother, the artist Jack Butler Yeats, did much of
the illustration work.

Dun Emer Logo.

Elinor Mary Darwin (1879–1954) was an Irish born illustrator,
engraver and portrait painter. Her illustrations were included in
several of her husband, Bernard Darwin's books for children.

Dun Emer Press was revived in 2008.

1

Metal

Metal

Pat and Mary Ryan were going to celebrate their golden wedding anniversary in just three weeks. Pat wanted a quiet enjoyable weekend in the place where they had spent their honeymoon. Mary was planning a big fancy party with fifty candles on a cake and all the trimmings in the hotel where they had held the wedding reception. She was getting stressed with the fact that more than half the invited guests were unable to make it. Some would have been over a hundred years old now if they hadn't passed away. Many more had moved too far away to attend.

Three weeks before the big day, Mary went into the garden to tidy the flowerbeds with Jack the terrier amusing her with his playfulness.

"Good boy, Jack," she said. While patting the dog she stared at her hand.

"Oh Jesus, please!" she called out. Her wedding ring, which had been on her finger for fifty years had gone! She searched the whole garden, even opened the compost bin, taking out all the weeds and deadheads she had just thrown in. There was no sign of the ring.

"Pat! Pat!" She ran into the house in a panic.

"What now?" Her husband saw tears welling up in her eyes. She told him she had lost her wedding ring.

"This is a bad sign," she said.

"Don't be silly, we'll find it." Pat followed her into the garden. They turned over every leaf and every pebble they could see. The wedding ring had vanished. Mary

Ryan was in bitter distress.

"We can't go anywhere now," she wailed, "I can't go to our honeymoon place together without my ring. People may think we're on a dirty weekend."

"Ah, you're crazy, people wouldn't even look." That night Mary prayed to Saint Anthony to help her find her ring.

"You know what, Mary?"

"What, Pat?" Pat had an idea.

"I'll ask Brian Butler. He may be able to help."

"Oh him, he's always full of drink, how is he supposed to help."

"He's got one of those yokes, I've seen him with it," explained Pat, "a yoke that finds anything made of metal."

In the morning before the pubs were open, Pat Ryan visited Brian Butler and promised to buy him a drink if he would lend him his metal detector.

Pat and Mary spent hours scanning their garden, getting many false alarms. The device bleeped and they found a rusty nail. It bleeped again at a 2 cent coin, then a bit of old wire and more nails. Jack, the little terrier jumped up and down impatiently.

"He wants his walk," said Pat.

"He has to wait," insisted Mary. The metal detector bleeped at the dog's collar and Pat switched off the device. Jack, startled by the noise ran over to the apple tree and lifted his leg. Next he squatted down and did the other business. Mary got the shovel from the shed.

"Jesus! Pat!"

"What now, Mary?"

"I've found it! I've found it!" She exclaimed with the excitement of a little girl.

"Oh, thank God, I've got it back!"

"Where was it? We looked everywhere!"

"Jack must have eaten it yesterday and…"

The following night Pat Ryan kept his promise and bought Brian Butler a drink. Some of Pat's neighbours were in the pub listening with interest and amusement to the story he had to tell.

2

Adventurous Journey

Adventurous Journey

The train stopped abruptly, as the barrier went up. All the passengers looked out the window to see what was going on. Last week there had been a bridge here. Now the tracks just stopped by the river.

"What now?" I asked.

"The train has to go back," said Andy.

"That means we won't get home before dark." Andy shrugged.

"Doesn't matter, we'll get there." My cousin was always so laid back. He had managed to get through any major upheaval and come out the other end like he had just woken up from a dream.

"Where's the bridge gone?" I insisted.

"It's broken," explained Andy. "They're going to fix it, see?" I could make out some workmen by the river. It could take a long time to repair that bridge, currently a pile of stones and rubble.

"Is the light still on in the tunnel?"

"Yes, I think so, but the train can't go through the tunnel."

"Why not?"

"Because it's on the other side of the river, silly! The bridge is just being fixed."

"I'm not silly." I scowled.

"Yes, you are, you know the train can't go through the water."

I'm going to show you, clever clogs! So I picked up the model train and placed it on the tracks over on the other side.

"There," I said, grinning at my cousin. Andy was determined to have the last laugh and pushed the button to bring down the barrier.

3

Tomorrow Never Comes

Tomorrow Never Comes

Someone with a warped sense of wisdom once told me that when you're up to the ears in shit the best you can do is turn it into fertiliser. Well, I should be able to make flowers grow in the desert.

On the same day that the call centre job didn't come off I received another email from this man called Richard. He had written to me before in reply to my ad, explaining that he ran his own recruitment business finding jobs for people, especially those new to Ireland. He wanted someone to keep his house tidy, maybe do a bit of cooking and help with some secretarial work. That's ideal! The website was odd, as it was all in French. I tried to read some people's messages on the site and could piece some bits together, as it's easier to understand written French than listening to someone speaking very fast with a regional accent. One emailer complained that the recruitment agency had promised him a job within a couple of days and he was still waiting after six weeks. This could have alarmed me, but I dismissed it, because, first, the man lived in a remote part of West Ireland where there weren't many jobs, and second, I was going to be a housekeeper and admin help and not just a recruitment agency client.

A nagging little voice in my head told me to be careful and I silenced it. My intuition, which used to be alert and very reliable, was taking a long holiday.

In his second email on Monday Richard explained a little about the work involved, and asked me to come for an interview to see the setup. I enquired at both the railway station and the bus station how to get from Cork to Enniscorthy and back. The trains are very awkward, all going to Dublin, and the bus journey takes a long time, especially since you have to change at Waterford and wait around there for over an hour. It was really only worth it if I was sure of a job, so I phoned Richard and explained the situation.

"It's great to hear an English voice," he said in a London accent. He was mainly dealing with Eastern Europeans. It turned out that he came from the same part of London where I had grown up and we chatted about some night spots we had both known. I tried to put a face to the voice. Thin, dark hair, glasses perhaps, thirty something. My stay at the Youth Hostel was paid for until Friday morning and I had to wait until then to move, as I couldn't get a refund.

"Okay, come up on Friday and we'll have a chat about everything. Even if you feel that keeping house for us isn't for you, you can stay as long as you like and I can get you a job within a few days – it's what I do."
I was a little sad at the thought of leaving Cork, as I had really got to like it there and I was only just beginning to find my way round the lively vibrant city. I had applied for none less than 39 jobs in just under two weeks, which proves that there are a lot of vacancies, as well as a lot of people after them. Had I had the cash to get through another week or two, I would have stayed on and may well have found the perfect job in time, but by Thursday

all I had left was 30 euros, which I needed for the trip the next morning. I said 'goodbye' to everyone, sorted the necessary paperwork and visited the internet café once more, to email my new address to a couple of people.

Packing your belongings is boring and travelling with a van load of luggage is a nightmare. After a rushed breakfast, I packed my lunch and other food stuff into a carrier bag attached to my handbag and waited impatiently for a taxi, which of course was stuck in the traffic. I checked the time on my mobile every two seconds. I'm going to miss the wretched bus! Well, the taxi arrived just in time.

That Friday it rained non-stop all day long. Waterford Bus Station is an icebox with automatic doors at both ends constantly flying open letting in arctic drafts. After waiting around there for over an hour I was sure that my feet were going to freeze off. The countryside on the way maybe beautiful on a sunny day, but observed through grey rain it's as interesting as looking at other people's family photos in black and white. I couldn't wait to get into that hot bath I had been looking forward to since Monday.

There is no bus station in Enniscorthy, just a bus stop in the middle of town. There were two men waiting at the bus stop and I had a certain picture in my head and promptly picked the wrong one. Henry VIII in a suit and tie, an inch or so shorter than me and 3ft wider, stepped out and said:

"Hi, I'm Richard!" He had greasy hair of a

nondescript colour, sort of dark grey, and smelled of liberally splashed on cheap aftershave. Was he really a successful businessman with pots of money? Maybe, one of those Londoners who worked himself out of a rough and tough family and did well in life, but had no idea what the rich and classy looked or smelled like. A shy little man introduced as Ramos sat in the passenger seat and I got in the back. The old rust bucket of a car with tangled seat belts and a jammed back door didn't speak of money either. I began to get suspicious.

"By the way," explained Richard, "the boiler is broken in the house. There's no heating and no hot water, but I got a little electric portable fire, which gets hot very quickly. The boiler will be fixed on Monday." So, I have to wait another three days for my much longed for hot bath. Ramos didn't speak until I mentioned in conversation that I had a cat and Richard immediately said:

"I hate cats."

"Why?"

"Horrible dirty flea ridden things."

"Cats aren't dirty," I came to their defence, "they always clean themselves and if you look after them properly they don't get fleas."

"They always got fleas. I'm a dog man."

"I like dogs, too, but in general cats are cleaner than dogs and easier to look after. And dogs can get fleas too."

"I love dogs," Ramos spoke for the first time, "and

I like cats, too." I wasn't going to introduce my cat to either of them, and let it drop.

Richard opened the door to the giant fridge freezer he called home and showed me the ice compartment which was going to be my bedroom. He put the little electric fire in the sitting room and we chatted about all sorts of things. He poured himself a vodka and served me and Ramos with a Bailey's.

"You can finish that stuff. I can't stand it. What do you normally drink?"

"Mainly red wine, though I quite like Irish whiskey occasionally."

"You're joking!" Why would I be? I had noticed that there were no pictures on the walls in any of the rooms and all the shelves and cabinets were empty. The door to my bedroom didn't shut properly and neither did the bathroom door. It came as no surprise when Richard told me that he was going to move shortly.

"But don't worry, it won't take me long to find something better and you can move with us as a housekeeper. Some people are coming to look at the house on Sunday and if they like it, we'll all be moving some time next week." Nobody is going to like a freezing house!

"Could you sell it so quickly?"

"This isn't my house, I rent it. But I own two houses out in the sticks, which I let out." I frowned. Why would anyone do that? Richard poured himself another vodka and moved on to talk about his business again.

"I don't do drugs, I don't do pornography, but I do some business which people may not always consider quite legal." I frowned again.

"I make at least 2,000 euros a week, usually more. If I take you on as a secretary you will make big money, 1,000 euros every week." That'll be the day!

"I'm happy to keep your house tidy and to do some typing or answering the phone and so on, but I'll tell you straight: I won't be getting involved in anything illegal."

"You don't have to, you can just do the ironing, but if you want to make big money..." He got up and put on a c.d. of some tuneless electric sound and then asked me what sort of music I liked.

"I like Irish music."

"You're joking." Why should I be joking? He doesn't like Irish whiskey, or Irish music – he doesn't have any Irish friends (if he has any friends at all), what is he doing here?

"I haven't got any Irish music. Oh yes, wait a minute..." Well, I suppose Ronan Keating is Irish music, though not the sort I meant, but definitely better than that electric stuff. Ronan Keating always reminds me of a lovely cruise holiday, as they were forever playing that c.d. on the ship.

"Tomorrow never comes..." Richard started singing along to it, his voice matching his sickly aftershave. Ramos came to the rescue.

"I don't like your presentation." Richard stopped abruptly and decided:

"I'm going to get some more booze. It's the weekend and we should all relax." Before he went out he changed the c.d. to some rap – and I was supposed to relax to that!

"I like Elton John," said Ramos, "I have several of his d.v.d.'s." He played one of them.

Richard soon returned with a bottle of red wine and a litre of vodka. He boasted that the bottle of wine was given to him by a friend who was a millionaire.

"That's my present to you," he said, "this is a very rare and very expensive bottle of wine, you know that? It costs 500 euros. My friend got two of them, and he gave me one, and I'm giving it to you."

"Thank you." Likely story!

"My friend is very well known all over Ireland."

"What's his name?"

"Doesn't matter." He kept knocking back the vodka like it was water and carried on telling big fish stories.

"I'm going to get a new house in a few days, don't worry. I'll pay cash for it."

"Where is your computer?" I tried to change the subject slightly.

"We don't keep one here now, we haven't got broadband and the landline is disconnected too, as we will soon be moving." The moving bit was probably the only true bit. He started playing rap and garage crap again and Ramos hated it as much as I did.

"Do you like Abba? Or Queen?"

"Yes, anything of the seventies." Richard turned to Ramos.

"Elton John! Queen! They're all bloody queers! Why do you like all that if you're not one of them?"

"I like the music and the good performance."

"Yes, I do too." He didn't listen to me.

"It's my house and I play the music I like!" He put on a c.d. of Frank Sinatra, dull but tolerable – Elton, Eminem, Sinatra, a strange mixture. It was Ramos' turn to speak.

"You brought another stranger to the house," he looked at Richard and then at me. "I don't like strangers in the house. They give away our secrets."

"I can keep a secret. If you ask me not to tell, I won't."

"I don't know you, you could be MI5, I don't know." I laughed.

"Don't tell her anything, Ramos." Richard's voice sounded threatening. He stormed out of the room to go to the loo. Storyteller! Drama Queen!

"Don't do the ironing tomorrow," Ramos whispered, "ask him to get you a job in a hotel or somewhere, tomorrow. He won't give you any business."

"I know he hasn't got a business that makes 2,000 euros a week, I know that's crap and that bottle of wine is probably from Tesco's. But, what about the housework?" Ramos shook his head.

"Don't do any housework. He's not going to pay you. He never pays anyone anything. Sometimes he gets people to pay him. When I was living in Brazil…" He quickly changed the subject, when he heard footsteps coming towards the room and talked in detail about life in Brazil.

"Good to see you're getting on really well." Richard grinned. "I know you'll be best friends by Monday. That's good, because I need you to look after Ramos while I'm away. I travel a lot and he needs someone to cook and clean up after him and I'll pay you good money for it." Yes, and I'm a man! Ramos pulled a face and Richard's tone changed suddenly.

"What have you been plotting behind my back?"

"Nothing. I was telling her about Brazil." Ramos was very nervous and I wondered whether he really was Portuguese, or was he Brazilian and staying here illegally, which made him so wary of strangers? I wouldn't shop a decent person just for being an illegal immigrant, but I would report a criminal who organised an illegal business. Richard was angry and very drunk and unpredictable.

"Go to bed, Ramos!"

"No, we were just having a conversation."

"Go to bed, both of you!"

"Don't tell me when to go to bed," I objected.

"This is my house!" Didn't he say he was renting this house? He unplugged the electric fire and carried it into my bedroom. I wasn't likely to get to sleep in a freezing room where the door couldn't be shut properly. I didn't want to stay up and be shouted at either and when Richard deliberately knocked a glass of vodka off the table smashing it on the floor, he scared me.

I kept my clothes on in the bedroom for two reasons: First, because it was freezing and second, goodness knows what a mentally unstable man with his brains pickled in two pints of vodka may be capable of. I was not going to take chances and crawled under the icy covers fully dressed. About ten minutes later Richard appeared in the room and asked:

"Why don't you go to sleep?"

"Because I'm bloody freezing."

"You can't be cold with that thing going constantly." Robert pointed at the electric fire. "It's been on since you got here this afternoon, costing me a bloody fortune." He unplugged it and marched out of the room with it. I'm going to die of hypothermia if nothing worse. I got up, put on my coat and boots, grabbed the two smaller bags and sneaked up to the loo, pulled the chain so he wouldn't hear the floor boards creaking, but when I came out of the bathroom, Richard stood there in shorts and t-shirt and demanded:

"Where are you going?"

"It's too cold to go to sleep, so I'm going for a walk." He shook his head, turned the key in the front door and placed it on the shelf, then banged at Ramos' bedroom door and yelled:

"Ramos! Ramos!" A minute later the little Portuguese opened the door.

"What do you want? I am tired."

"Ramos, sort this woman out!"

"What do you mean?"

"Sort her out! She can't just leave the house in the middle of the night." I was really scared now, but did my best to keep my head straight. The presence of Ramos made me feel a little safer, although he was small and thin and tired, but at least I wasn't alone in the house with a madman.

"Ramos, please tell your mate here not to come into my bedroom." The five-year-old trapped in a forty-year-old body threw a tantrum.

"This is my house! I can go in what room I want!" "I'm leaving tomorrow," said Ramos. I had no choice but to go back into my bedroom and waited for Richard to return to his. I heard the electric fire blowing next door and on impulse I sent a text to Dave. Not sure how he could possibly help over that distance, but his reply was a comfort. I didn't even know if the emergency number would be the same 999 here as in the U.K. Richard had heard the text jingle and came into the room again.

"You didn't call the police, did you?"

"What by text? No, only my husband."

"Go to sleep!"

"How can I, if you keep coming into my room?" He left and ten minutes later he returned. He talked a lot of drunken rubbish and walked to the middle of the room. I was terrified of what he might do next.

"Would you please go to your own room? It just isn't done walking into a woman's bedroom like that." Every ten minutes or so, when I thought he had finally gone to bed, he was back in my room again. This was repeated about five times, until he finally left me in peace – by no means at peace, and I lay there shivering and shaking with my eyes pinned on the door. Every half hour or so I checked the time on my mobile phone and Ronan Keating was crooning in my head appropriately: Tomorrow never comes...

Next door, Richard was snoring like a dragon and definitely fast asleep now, though I worried, whenever I couldn't hear the snoring for two minutes, that he was awake and walking into my room again. 2.34... 2.58... 3.29... ... I could really believe that tomorrow would never come. 6.21... 6.43... 7.12... the dragon was still sleeping, when I got up, put on my boots, took my handbag and the case containing the laptop, went to the loo and made for the front door. I turned the key quietly and slipped out along the garden path, through the broken gate into the road. How many strange dreams have I had where I was trapped in a house and had to find a way out without being seen? And how many hundreds of dreams have I had of carrying luggage through a deserted unknown town at an antisocial hour, not knowing where I was going? I was usually running away and hiding from someone in alleyways, looking behind me to make sure I wasn't being followed. He may be following me in the car and every old rust bucket going past was a suspect. All the shops were shut and I asked an old lady walking her dog, if there was a café open and there wouldn't be for at least another half hour. The road works started their day at first light and a large part of the town centre was closed to traffic, which added to the dreamlike atmosphere. I began to look for a café and I also needed to find a police station to report the events of that dreadful night and wondered if I would ever see my big heavy luggage and its contents again. An old man plodding along an otherwise lifeless road was the only person to approach. He was hard to understand, as he had no teeth at all, but he was helpful. He walked to the Garda Station with me and when I told him part of my story he said:

"If you can't find anywhere else you can stay with me for a couple of nights." Although he was very old and probably quite alright, I was not going to take any more risks. I described my escape and the events leading up to it in detail to the Gardai and they bent over backwards to help me. While I waited Richard sent a text.

"I want to talk." He had a nerve expecting me to call him on my expensive UK phone. I had nothing more to say to him, as he wasn't likely to listen anyway. Another text arrived.

"I am leaving shortly, what do I do with your stuff?" I replied that I was going to send someone to pick it up. Two officers – one male, one female – got into a car with me and drove towards the house, which I recognised by the broken gate. They retrieved my two big suitcases while I waited in the car. Apparently Richard behaved in a civilised manner (he was probably too nervous to be rude to the police) and Ramos was not present. I suggested that they keep an eye on Richard, though of course I had no evidence for his dodgy business, except his word.

I waited ages at the Garda Station and went for a much longed for cup of coffee at the nearest café. The two helpful officers had tried to book me into a hostel in Wexford, which was full and after phoning around found one in Kilkenny. They gave me and my belongings a lift to the bus stop with a handwritten note for the driver to let me travel without a ticket.

I am sure I have at least one guardian angel, who protected me that night. Angels are protectors as much as challengers putting us to the test, and they are not saints. The worst part of the long journey was having to change buses at Waterford Bus Station, waiting three hours there and getting frozen to the bone. Without the helpful people there, I may not have found the right bus. If I had not been so cold, I may have dozed off on the bus to Kilkenny and missed my stop, as I was so dog-tired, with a sleepless night catching up on me. By the time I reached the hostel it was dark. It didn't matter what time it was. I wasn't even hungry and too tired for a bath. Now everything can wait until tomorrow, when tomorrow comes!

4

Lost in Translation

Lost in Translation

Mercedes was twenty-one when she came over from Spain to London to work as an au-pair. She had travelled before, around Europe, but never stayed away from home for so long. A whole year to improve her English and to get used to very different food. The latter was not so easy.

Mercedes was an animal lover, a campaigner in Spain to end bull fighting and other blood sports. She was delighted when part of her work as an au-pair included walking the family dog. She and the pet became the best of friends. Mercedes had not yet had the pleasure of meeting the family's cat, who apparently came and went and did not often stay in the house. The children were well behaved and their father was often out at work. The mother was an old-fashioned English middle class housewife, who, in her spare time made cakes for the W.I. and enjoyed knitting toys. Mercedes was comfortable with the family until some day, the mother announced:

"We will all be out this afternoon. You can dust and hoover the front room. I have a lovely gateau in the fridge. Help yourself to a piece or two."

The Spanish girl looked shocked, when the woman left her alone in the house. There was not much work to be done and she made herself a coffee, but could not bring herself to open the fridge for the milk. So she had her coffee black and sat out in the garden, when a little tabby cat came up to her, purring. She patted the animal and spoke in Spanish. When the cat tried to follow her into the house, Mercedes shut the door. She poured herself another black coffee, unable to relax with the woman's voice in her head "I have a lovely gateau in the fridge…" She looked at the cat, with tears in her eyes.

When the family returned, the cat came running into the house. The mother picked it up, cooing at it, as Mercedes looked on horrified.

"I know what you want," said the woman to the cat, "you want some cream." She opened the fridge and took out the cream cake.

"Oh Mercedes, you didn't have a piece of gateau, would you like some now?"

Gateau = a cream cake;
El gato = (Spanish) a cat.

5

Gone Bananas

Gone Bananas

We were living in stressful times, when money and patience were running out fast and people in public places were getting uptight about the slightest little misunderstanding. I liked buying my fruit and vegetables from a market stall rather than at the supermarket, the only disadvantage being that they didn't always let you choose your own. You would ask for a pound of tomatoes and they would quickly pop them into a paper bag, put it on the scales and say:

"That's thirty pence for you, madam." You would pay and they would hand over the goods and when you got home you would usually find a couple of manky squashed tomatoes at the bottom of the bag.

There were nearly always too many bananas to a bunch and I only bought them if I could pick my own to make sure they didn't sneak a brown squishy one into the bag. While both sellers at the fruit stall were serving customers I had a good look at the bananas which were all in bunches of fours and fives. I took a bunch of four, broke one off and handed the remaining three to the woman.

"What's wrong with that one?" she demanded, pointing at the one I had put back. Before I could say nothing, but I only want three and not four she held the bunch of three in one hand and the lone banana in the other and shook her head.

"I can't see anything wrong with this, can you, Jim?" She showed the bananas to her husband.

"Can you see anything wrong with that banana?" Like me Jim couldn't get a word in edgeways. The woman turned the fruit around in her hand so I would see it from all angles.

"It's perfectly alright! So why did you put this one back?" Next, she began to peel the banana and again turned it around for me to see that it was flawless, then took a bite and handed it to her husband.

"It's absolutely fine, innit, Jim? There's nothing wrong with that banana at all!" Jim felt he had no choice but to taste it, then gave it back with the verdict:

"It's fine."

"There you are, I told you so." The woman was talking to all the customers at the stall now. "Some people are just so fussy." Jim handed me the bunch of three. I gave him forty pence and whispered:

"I only wanted three." He nodded.

"Give it a rest, Joan."

"No," she argued stridently, "out of principle, I won't. I mean, look at all them bananas, they're all perfect. We don't sell bad ones." I heard her carry on from quite a few yards away.

"I just can't believe some people! They want everything like it's painted."

"Yeah," said Jim, "they'll be asking for straight ones next."

Extract from: "Woman Trouble" (autobiographical novel)

6

The Sign of the Lion

The Sign of the Lion

Anna's baby was due in a week. She returned from a visit to her sister with a bag full of nappies, towels and other small necessities. She walked from the bus stop with mixed feelings in the sweltering heat, when finding herself totally alone in the street. "Home in a min, love you" she texted her husband, but the message could not be sent. She felt too hot in long sleeves and long skirt, with her hair tied back in a ponytail. Her heart thumped when she stepped into her house through a broken front door. Her home had been ransacked. Her next door neighbours had also fled. Anna knew something terrible had happened. Her husband and his parents would not have gone anywhere without her. They had been taken prisoner, along with their neighbours, and most likely murdered.

She stood trembling in what used to be her sitting room among a heap of broken furniture, when her waters broke. She crouched on the floor and prayed. Her prayers were answered, when the birth of her daughter was easy and natural without complications and the child was healthy and strong. Anna did everything herself, with her faith in God and her qualifications as a nurse. She wrapped the baby in a towel and carried her in one arm and the bag in the other. The bottle of water was heavy, but absolutely essential.

The whole street was eerily deserted, further along with many buildings bombed and ruined. With her phone not working, communication was not possible.

She somehow had to return to her sister's house on foot, avoiding the main streets and public transport.

It was getting dark, when Anna arrived at the corner of the street, where her sister lived. She had not met another human being on her long walk. Then she heard voices by the church over the road, shouting and screaming, and loud engine noises. She hardly dared to look at the church she knew so well and whispered a prayer. There was an explosion and rocks flew in the air, a cross, half a shattered window, bits of glass, flames reaching up to the sky.

Anna moved by instinct, into the alley behind her, like an animal. She soothed the crying baby and fed her, while walking through empty ruined buildings, stumbling over stones and debris along winding lanes, trying to make her way out of the destroyed city. She sat on a rock behind a large wall that had once belonged to a shop to gather her thoughts, again feeding the baby and using another nappy. She needed to get out of the bombed district, yet knew that she was safer there than among people. She trusted in God to guide her to safety, as he had done so far. Time didn't matter anymore. It made no difference whether it was morning or afternoon, or which day of the week it was. The darkness of the night increased the danger a little, while the day was long and hot. The child was still gaining strength, although her mother was exhausted. Anna had to find food for herself, or her milk would run dry and her tiny daughter would starve. She couldn't think of the past, not even the immediate past. Even tomorrow was a million years away. No time to mourn her family, no time to plan a future. No time to feel sick, or sad or scared, only to have an instinct to protect her baby and to survive.

Somehow she had to find her way to the harbour and try to get on a ship and out of the war torn country. There was nothing left here now, except danger. She had been walking for what seemed like forever, carrying her newborn baby. She could not risk sleep. She had to keep her eyes open. Everything she saw, heard, sensed was suspicious and potentially dangerous. Every light could be a distant explosion and every rat in the rubble a spy. Anna drank from the water bottle, which had got warm, but she would save the last drop for as long as possible. She looked up at the sky. The stars were particularly bright and the constellation of Leo was clearly visible – the sign of power and strength. Her heavy eyes fell shut and she was in her soft warm bed with her husband beside her, smiling at the baby. Then he faded away. Anna opened her eyes and immediately got to her feet. Although her body was aching, she felt she had gained a little more energy and new encouragement. How long had she rested? Five minutes? An hour? Two hours? It didn't matter. The sun was rising, lighting her path. Birds flew above the ruins – here and there a vulture, then sea gulls – the harbour was not far. In the cool early morning breeze a bright coloured cloth tumbled down to her feet. Blue and red and green and yellow. Anna picked it up and looked around. Whoever had lost this could not be far. Anna wrapped her baby in the scarf, as she walked towards the harbour lights.

***

Amina switched on the morning news, as soon as she heard her husband's car drive away to his work. Until last week she had had a job as a clerk in a bank, then the bank closed 'for some political reason.' Her husband threatened her, though of course it was not her fault. She believed it was only temporary, until everything was a bit more settled, whenever that would be.

Amina and Ahmad had been married five years. The first year or so had been ok. When Amina found out that she was unable to have children, her husband changed. It started with name calling and unpleasant gestures, developing into full physical abuse. Nobody saw the bruises on her body – nobody asked questions. The last time, he had beaten her, she challenged him.

"Go on then, hit me in the face." He hesitated. He threw a shoe at her and stormed out of the house. He would not hit her where everyone could see the evidence. When she lost her job, she was not so sure. His anger increased. He got angry with his work, with the unstable political situation, with so many things, and everything was his wife's fault. He let all his anger out on her. Then he even turned on Amina's grandmother, calling her a lazy and useless parasite, although it was her who kept the house clean and tidy while both he and Amina were out at work. Amina began to plan her escape a while ago, when she saw on social media what the censored news on television wouldn't show. People were leaving the country in droves. The danger came closer each day. When the bank shut down, she had no reason to stay. It took a while to persuade her grandmother. The old lady was set in her ways, although she had known better days, more liberal times. As a young woman Afia had worn modern fashions and hair styles. Until recently you could still buy stylish dresses and high heeled shoes in High Street stores. Now, politics were travelling too far back in time. She often looked at the photos on Amina's laptop with nostalgia. She was wary of leaving her home to start again in a strange country. Amina encouraged her that she "could have all this again."

That morning they both watched the news on television, until a fuse blew and no signal was found for the internet. Ahmad was at work and Amina packed two carrier bags with bread and cheese, bottled water and some small necessities. The two women shut the front door behind them.

"Where are we going?" Afia asked nervously.

"I don't know," said Amina, "away from here." They walked along the main road leading out of the city centre. Amina wondered how many of the thronging crowd and traffic were going the same way. It was best not to speak to, or trust any strangers. They stopped occasionally for a drop of water and a bit of bread and cheese.

The sun set and the temperature dropped. They sat on a bench with their minds full of racing thoughts. Neither was able to sleep, but they rested their tired feet. Later, as they walked along on a narrow path through a demolished street of a former Christian area, Amina remembered some customers at the bank with addresses here. It was not safe to carry on and they had to change direction and get out of town. They began to walk into a field. Here a fresh path had been created by the unmistakable marks of a tank. Amina shuddered and stared at the fresh tracks. She listened for clues of how far the tank had gone. She and her grandmother had to go in the opposite direction. At least the old woman had mellowed a little, since the pair had started on their journey, realising the danger they were in. Amina had seen the same pictures on the internet news, day after day, that were now right before her eyes. They ran, then hid behind a large rock to gather their thoughts. The harbour was not far now.

"They will see you, before they see me," Afia admonished Amina for wearing such bright colours. Amina had thought when getting dressed that morning. *If I have to wear those old fashioned clothes, at least I can wear pretty ones.* A rainbow coloured skirt with matching head scarf – the proper attire, though maybe her grandmother was right, that those colours could shine a light to her whereabouts. She took off the scarf and left it by the rock.

***

The harbour was closed to normal traffic. A ship was being prepared. People ran about, pushing and shoving, holding children and small bags. Men collected money and were robbed only a few feet away by other men.

Ragged, tired, dirty and desperate in the chaos of the harbour, to get on the ship to safety. There were always some individuals who turned the misfortune of others to their advantage.

"Did you bring money?" Afia whispered nervously. Amina nodded, clutching her bag.

"I have no money," a woman cried in anguish. Another woman pushed her and ordered her to the back of the already disorderly queue, without compassion. Anna looked over at the woman in the bright skirt, now very scared, saying a prayer in her head. Amina saw the tiny baby wrapped in what used to be her scarf and smiled. She paid the opportunist on the peer and said:

"She is with us."

"You pay her fare?" The man demanded. Before she could answer, the man was punched by another, who grabbed his bag of money.

"Now," said Amina, gesturing to Anna.

"I want to go home," her grandmother pleaded. Amina took her hand and pulled her up the step.

"Soon," she promised.

"My leg!" Afia screamed. She was in serious pain, though not the only one who got hurt while climbing up the rickety steps. There were too many people on the ship and still many more trying to get on. An announcement came through a loudspeaker that the ship was full to capacity and had to sail now.

Amina elbowed her way through the crowd. People huddled together on seats and on the floor, tired and dirty and afraid. Still some pushed and punched to get on and some had to be left behind to wait for the next ship. The heat was stifling.

"Will you please let my grandmother sit and rest," Amina pleaded. "She has hurt her leg. And please let the woman with the baby sit, too."

"Thank you so much, you're so kind," said Anna, as she took her place next to Afia. Now Amina could have a better look at the baby, peacefully asleep among the turmoil. Afia wailed with the throbbing pain. Anna offered to help.

"Can I see? I'm a nurse." She handed the baby to Amina to hold. There were men on the ship looking in their direction and the old woman refused to expose her leg in front of them. The chaos eased a little when the ship began to sail. Two young women in uniform handed out bread and fresh water to those most in need. Then two paramedics arrived, speaking English and French. Getting the injured old lady to a cabin to be examined seemed more of an upheaval than the long walk she had just undertaken with her granddaughter. Anna told them she was a nurse and happy to be of assistance. The portholes danced in front of her tired eyes and the floor under her feet gave way. The paramedic caught her and placed her on a bunk.

"Do you speak English?" he asked Amina, while the other paramedic examined Afia's leg.

"A little," Amina replied, "if you speak slowly."

"The doctor will be here soon," he explained. "The leg

wound will be cleaned and dressed and it won't need stitches. Do you need any help with your baby?"

"Yes, I will," Amina was confused. "Her mother fainted. Will she be alright?"

The paramedic nodded, thinking *dear God, this child can only be a couple of days old.*

"Yes, she is just exhausted. Please would you all stay in this cabin? All will be well." Sometimes good can come out of a bad situation. They were safe in the cabin. They had fresh water and bread and easy access to a bathroom. Who knows where they would be if Afia had not injured her leg. A female doctor examined and treated the old woman and a nurse attended to the baby.

Hours passed and the sun set when Anna came to. She looked around herself bewildered. *What happened? Where am I?* Was this a dream, or had she just woken from one? Afia lay asleep on the bunk with her skirt tied around her bandaged leg for extra support. Anna looked around. Her baby had no name yet. She had not been baptised and she was probably hungry. Anna had to find her immediately. The bathroom door opened and Amina stepped into the cabin with the baby girl asleep in her arms.

"She is fine," said Amina and carefully handed the baby back to her mother, "just tired."

"Thank you," said Anna, "you're very kind. You will be a good mother." Amina shook her head, holding back tears. The two women established trust between them and told their stories to each other. Anna looked through the porthole. It was dark and hard to distinguish the sea from the sky. Silver stars on a black background and the occasional spray on the glass of the porthole. The crescent moon swam past, then Anna found it.

"The sign of the lion!" She called out and stepped back to let Amina see it. Amina had never seen the stars so clear and bright. She had never looked at the sky in the same way that Anna had.

"If you see a shooting star, make a wish," said Anna enthusiastically. "I saw one last night." Her excited voice woke both the baby and the old woman. Afia smiled at her granddaughter and the young mother. None of them had any idea where the ship was going to berth and where they were going to live once they walked on land again. Anna's faith in God would help her make the right decisions. Her baby may grow up never knowing the country of her birth. She would speak a new language, that her mother would have to learn. Many things would be very different, but the moon and stars would be the same, as they can be seen anywhere in the world. Anna and Amina, although of the same age group, had grown up in different cultures and may not have met if they had not needed to flee their war torn country. But here they were in the same situation, with the same uncertainty ahead of them as everyone else on this ship. In a short time they had got to know and trust each other, and so began a long lasting friendship.

7

America

America

On honeymoon we had travelled from Washington DC to New York City on a greyhound bus. Everything is big in America – the roads, the buildings, some trucks as big as houses. I felt like a prime fool when I had asked someone what sort of bird was the one with the red chest.

"That's a robin!" I was told. Of course it is! I hadn't come across a pigeon during our stay and wondered whether American pigeons were the size of ravens. Sadly those giant robins never posed for my camera. We were caught in a hail shower, with hail stones the size of bricks, painfully refreshing, though the heat returned within minutes and the earth was dry again as if it had never happened.

We went in a hire car all through Virginia, the forest and the Blue Ridge Mountains, singing along:

"In the Blue Ridge Mountains of Virginia, on the trail of the lonesome pine..."

We couldn't find the 'lonesome pine', but saw some interesting places like ghost towns with churches of denominations I had never heard of before. Religion was prominent in the State. In Washington DC we had asked directions from a man in the street, which he obliged to give, followed by fundamentalist preaching of the Gospel of Atheism.

We abandoned our search for the 'lonesome pine' and stopped at a petrol station where hymns were playing on local radio, not only on a Sunday. I had seen those remote shops in many crime serials – something dangerous usually happened there. Luckily we didn't need condoms or tampons, as neither was on sale there, but we could probably have bought a gun if we wanted to. However, the people were generally very friendly and helpful.

We had lunch in a real life American diner in the middle of nowhere, likely the only visitors from overseas. I had my first ever iced tea – strange but not unpleasant. We were served a bag of crisps with our salad, when we ordered chips and realised we should have asked for 'French fries'. The staff there worked hard, frying burgers and sausages in the heat, while keeping a great sense of humour.

"Tomatoes!" The woman called to her colleagues, "he said tomatoes! That's so cute!" That song was going around in my head: I say tomatoes, you say tomaytoes... let's call the whole thing off...

Some shady characters were among the customers. Or was I thinking of the television series again? Did any of them have a gun in his pocket or leave it in the car? A rough looking man had been staring at me in an unnerving manner all through lunch. Walking out of the café holding my new husband's hand, didn't stop him from following us. I turned my back, ignoring him when his voice was right in my ear.

"You gonna have to do exactly as I tell you, or you'll be in real trouble." I grabbed my husband's hand tighter and quickened my pace, steering him towards the car.

"Let's get away from here," I said, "that man is up to something." We got into the car, parked next to some sort of small builder's truck and locked all the doors and windows. It was hot and stuffy inside and I could hardly breathe.

The man was still looking at me, when my husband started the engine. He slowly walked towards us. Then I noticed he was talking into his phone, when opening the door to his truck.

The Bulb

The Bulb

How many clumsy women does it take to change a light bulb? That really depends. How many psychologists does it take to change a light bulb? Only one, but the bulb really has to want to change. Now this one didn't, stubborn old thing just wouldn't budge. Those cheap things don't last five minutes and the dearer ones aren't bright enough. My neighbour was happy to help and turned the thing, though it still wouldn't come out.

"I think it needs a new fitting," he said, "and you'll need an electrician to do that. John from across the road does electrical work, maybe he can help."

"Thanks." I went to ask John and found out that he was on holiday for two weeks. I need a light in my sitting room tonight! Fierce determination might just do it. So I went back on the chair with a screw driver. That bulb must have welded itself to the fitting.

"Move, you bastard!" It wouldn't. The stress of trying only made me livid. Good job no-one could hear my selection of expletives. Anger can make you stronger and takes away fear. I squeezed with force and felt something move.

"Oh good, at last," I said to myself red-faced, only to find that the wretched bulb was broken and the other half of it was still stuck in the fitting. Now in pedestrian road rage I threw the glass and screw driver on the floor and flopped onto the sofa tearing at my hair.

"Bugger this!" I yelled, and as I touched the lampshade, the fitting fell to the floor.

9

Confinement

Confinement

Julie thought she had nearly got there. She always nearly got there. Was it really better to share a cell with some psycho or to be alone? In solitary confinement she could use her time to be creative. She could draw or write, provided she had enough paper and a good pencil.

Maggie was moved into a cell of her own after she had torn up Julie's drawings and used the pencil as a weapon. With a twisted face she held it up to her cellmate and threatened:

"I can stab you with this big strong point, just you watch it. It's got poison in it – lead, see that?" She held it up to Julie's face.

"Poison!" Poison was the reason Maggie was in jail. She had pleaded guilty, too.

"Yeah, I did it! I saw all the dead rats in the yard. So I put some of the stuff in his tea, as he was a rat. So now he can't cheat on me anymore."

Julie was relieved when Maggie was moved. It was quiet now, except for meal times and exercise, when she would have to see all the others. Maggie was handcuffed when she threatened an officer with cutlery.

Julie wrote in her diary and then she drew a picture of a beautiful landscape and a beautiful house, where she was going to live, when this was over. She would have it framed like she was framed. It was only a week to the next court case and she would win this time.

10

One Blade of Grass

One Blade of Grass

It was so long ago now – a whole generation or more. I was a girl of just seven summers, when I became aware that the life we had known and enjoyed was about to change forever. Everything the Old Wise One had foreseen has come to pass. I learned and I taught. I knew joy and I knew pain, intense love, hate, justice, injustice, war, peace, fear, courage, fun, suffering. I took and I gave, I shared and I kept some of the wisdom which is forever to remain secret. That which was forbidden was usually more interesting than what was allowed. While our tribe was not at war with anyone, there was no danger of being taken hostage or captured to be sold into slavery. We came across very few strangers when out playing. We saw peasants working in the fields and weren't allowed to go near them, their children or their dwellings. We didn't want to, as they frightened us. Some were so dirty and ugly, they terrified us. We might die of some horrible disease if they touched us. So many of their own young died. They were a different race, almost a different species, with their own beliefs, their own laws or lack of them. As a child I believed they were born with black hands and feet. Some surely were born with misshapen bodies or twisted faces. There were two main types of peasants: The strong and hard-working, who lived in families, did their best to keep within the law and even cleaned themselves and their dwellings. They worked in our fields, their children became our servants and some of their men fought in battles alongside our warriors. The other sort were the ones we feared – the misbegotten, who seemed to have no law. A wild animal could be tamed, while those creatures could never be trusted. It was said that brothers and sisters forgot who they were and bred with each other, giving birth to hideous disfigurements. It was the ugliness which scared us so. We heard stories of babies born with feet instead of hands; women with six breasts and men with two heads. We had no evidence of this, as we never saw such freaks. But the mere chance of meeting one, terrified us and we kept well away from their dwellings. Now, after all this time, this is almost laughable. It doesn't matter anymore who you are, which tribe you are born into, how much land or cattle you own. Now, it makes no difference whether you are a chieftain or a peasant, as everyone feels the same hunger pains, when there is nothing left to eat but grass. Something much worse than blackhanded peasants had come to ravage our land. They took everything from us and claimed it as their own. They devastated our forests and fields, poisoned our rivers and lakes. They occupied our towns, enslaved our children and forced us to pay a tax on our own possessions so high that we had to let it go. They wanted us to work for them to earn it back. They planted a new grain and made bread, which made many of us sick – likely the reason why they planted it. All their warriors are men, who look rather strange. Their hair is cut short and their faces clean shaven. Their legs are also short and they wear no breeches or boots, but peculiar leather straps tied across bare feet, around their ankles up to their knees, with metal soles. They have iron helmets on their heads and shirts made of chains, must be very heavy, yet still they fight fiercely. Another place we were forbidden to go was the forest. We could go to the fringe of it, and it was plain common sense not to wander off into the wildwoods and get lost. Not only a variety of dangerous wild animals lived in the woods, but also the Green Folk, the Shining Ones, dragons, goblins, giants and shape shifters. Some were said to be friendly, even helpful, others were known to abduct children who were never seen again, at least not in their usual shape. All this was far more intriguing than frightening. Shape shifting in particular, fascinated me, a skill I would have liked to learn.

Curiosity drove me to the forest, in the season of Samhain, the year end, when the veils between the worlds were thin. You were supposed to see, and even experience, things which you didn't see the rest of the year. Some said the gods came to the earthly realm to communicate. Priests and priestesses were extremely secretive about this communication.

I rode across the fields on my own, after deliberately losing my siblings and friends. I looked behind to check if they were following. They weren't. I let my horse slowly trot into the woods. Very few leaves were left on the trees, a lot more on the ground, which was wet from rain. Hazel nuts and elderberries had already been picked. Holly berries were green, soon to turn red. Ivy creeping up ancient long dead trunks made them appear alive again. Mist was rising like water. I must have been three years old when I first heard the story of the wood under water… "To reach the Land of the Dead beneath the vast eternal sea, you must go through the realm of the mist and find your way through the wood under water…" No-one returned from the Otherworld the same way they went in. It's where the souls of the dead go to be healed and cleansed, then to be reborn into another body. The souls of the ancient wise ones live in the trees. But so much else lived in the woods. I carried on deeper into the forest. The atmosphere changed as I came out of the familiar wood of ash, oak, hawthorn and elder entering an area predominated by birch trees. This lent it a more ethereal quality. Anyone may expect a forest to get darker the deeper it gets, but the birches seemed to light it up. Maybe this was the realm of the Shining Ones and perhaps the wood under water wasn't far now. The path gradually disintegrated and I could ride no further. I dismounted and tied the horse to a tree. I began to wind my way through the bushes. It was eerily quiet. The occasional bird or squirrel rustled high up – there was nothing on the ground. My own heartbeat and footsteps – not even the trees creaked, as they often did in the wind. The birches stood upright and white like tall slender women – giant women. One enormous great ash, branches reaching up into infinity picking the stars from the sky. Two queenly beeches at his side – one leaning over to advise him. Here and there a few hawthorns and hazels, brown ferns asleep under fallen leaves, and so many brambles. Their thorns tore at my clothes. My skirt was soaked like a sponge up to the waist. Dead leaves and twigs clung to it and got caught in my hair. Anyone may believe I had been to the wood under water, being wet enough. Faces in the trees - some urging me to go home, others inviting me to move on.

I walked on. The birches were getting fewer and gradually being replaced by beech and ash with the occasional oak. One oak tree was as big as a house and hollow inside. It was pitch black. There were brambles in the way. I was trying to work out a way of entering the tree, without being scratched. I looked behind me for anything to stand on and discovered a clearing I hadn't noticed before. A manmade clearing, circular, the size of a small house, only a few paces away. In the centre was a burnt patch, where a fire had been some time ago – not a cooking fire. There were no footprints human or animal. Brambles had reclaimed the path, if ever there had been one.

Determination found a way. Carefully I trod on the brambles creaking under my feet, and entered the circle. I stood in the middle on the ashes. The energy felt sinister – or was it just awesome? I looked eastward at the great hollow oak. There was something menacing about that tree. He was watching me. Something… everything was watching me. I felt a thousand eyes on me. A crow took flight warning of battles – even Morganu left this place. I wasn't meant to be here.

In the west the ghostly evening sun poured through

leafless branches onto the ground like blood. The sun mortally wounded was to die at the year end... Then a light, an ugly yellow flame, a gleaming iron sword of gigantic proportions cut through the forest. It virtually cut the forest in half and created a path a good thirty paces wide and endless long. Lightning flashed and set the trees on fire. A tidal wave from the north swept the ashes. The sound of horses and the terrible yell of men charging into battle. A crash! I screamed. Silence. I stared at the sunset. There was nothing. The trees were unchanged and unharmed. My heart thumped. I had to get away from this place as fast as I could. Disregarding brambles and thorns and painful scratches, I ran.

All out of breath I arrived in the birchwood. Thank goodness my horse was still there. I was trying to think of a believable story to tell my parents. There was no need. As I approached the mare, she reared up.

"Don't worry," I said, "I'm going to untie you and we're going home." She stood on her hindlegs. She was angry, perhaps for leaving her tied to a tree for so long. I jumped aside to avoid being trampled on. She turned her head and neighed at me, still standing upright. Then I realised I must have brought a terrible energy with me from the circle. Animals are sensitive – my horse picked up that energy and it frightened her. I tried to calm her, talking in a soothing voice. She snorted. She gave me a really strange look – uneasy, as well as stubborn. When she came back on all fours, I quickly untied the knot and grabbed the reins, using all my strength to hold her down.

Slowly I managed to reach a hand onto the saddle, but the moment I was going to mount, the mare reared up again. I fell. She bolted. I had to let her go. She galloped in the direction of home.

When I arrived home, it was almost dark. My mother stood in the porch waiting for me, with a grave look on her face.

"Where on earth have you been?" she asked. I couldn't answer that, not sure if I had been on earth at all.

I was grounded for many days, allowed only a few paces outside the house to play, unless accompanied by an adult. This was a fitting lesson for my irresponsible actions and I accepted it. But at night I could find no rest, plagued with dreams and nightmares of the men of iron.

As children, we spent little time in the house generally – our favourite games were only possible outdoors. We played races on horseback or on foot. "See who's first down the hill" was a favourite. We played hide and seek and more often we played battles. This involved role playing and we took turns in playing our people or our enemies. We put a lot of drama into it. But we always knew we were acting. We used long sturdy wooden sticks for swords, some cut and carved into the right shapes, longer ones for spears, and had to be very careful with those weapons. Toy shields were made from animal skins, leather or light wood, which sometimes got damaged. We even had proper leather sheaths for our toy swords. We didn't wear special costumes, as we changed roles too often, and of course didn't put on our best clothes for rough games. There were many tools we weren't allowed to use. Real weapons were out of the question, so were cooking utensils, except old wooden spoons and broom handles. Many of our wooden sword sticks got broken during such a game. Bruises and splinters and ripped clothes were too commonplace. We had been at peace with our neighbours for so long now, that no-one under the age of nine had ever witnessed a real battle.

I loved being a warrior thrashing into the hedges with my wooden sword stick, pretending rocks on the ground were enemies, and screaming a blood-curdling battle cry. We stuffed pieces of old cloth with straw and pebbles, tied them up with string more like effigies than dolls, with straw or grass for hair. Sometimes we found bits of wool in the hedgerow, small leaves and moss to make a crude face. Sword fights were fun and good practice should it ever be necessary. We held captives for ransom and confiscated jewellery, which after the game was returned to the rightful owners. We always came away with cuts and bruises and in wintry weather covered in mud. We let our imagination run wild, since most of us only knew about battles from stories. We heard stories of the Old Ones, the Shining Ones, the Green Folk and many heroes. They were to be respected and only the Men of Iron were never to be trusted. These were the new enemies and we were soon to find out that they were at least as bad, if not worse than what we had imagined. Many a boy or girl was warned not to wander too far from home into dangerous territory where they may be captured by the Men of Iron, never to be seen again. The Green Folk may carry you away through the wildwoods into another world, but taken by the men of iron you were lost forever.

In a variation of a battle game, we could wield swords more forcefully, aim spears and shoot catapults directly, as we were fighting an invisible enemy. This meant all of us were warriors, hiding in the hollows disguised as trees. More true to life we were defending our town, throwing stones and toy spears over hedges and earthworks. Animals ran to the other end of their enclosures to be safely out of our way.

We decided to fight the Men of Iron and defend our town. We rubbed earth on our faces, put moss on our heads and lay under a blanket of twigs and leaves, waiting by the earthworks, looking down the path across the fields. The atmosphere was tense and my heart thumped. I knew the Men of Iron would be coming. The old wise woman had predicted troubled times ahead. I heard nothing but my own heartbeat – the silence was eerie. The air was cold, yet there was no wind. From our position we could see far beyond the fields, while no-one could see us. Earthworks were designed to hide behind and surprise the enemy. I saw nothing.

Suddenly an icy gust of wind blew from north-west out of town. The hedges seemed to shiver and as I blinked a chain of iron-clad men lined the edge of the earthworks. I yelled a battle cry. We all threw spears and shot sling stones. The Men of Iron ran over us against the wind into the town. My gaze fixed on one quivering blade of grass as I felt a stabbing pain in my chest and fell. One blade of grass stood upright like a sword, withstanding the trampling of these strange iron-soled shoes. It grew before my eyes taller than myself. Everyone continued yelling and screaming, waving swords and throwing spears and stones into the hedges. The Men of Iron vanished and the world turned black.

I was half aware of being carried – through the clouds I thought – into the Underworld by a queen. I woke with my head buried in a huge bosom, my legs supported by a pair of fat arms. My eyes opened slowly and met Elned's shocked expression.

"What happened?" she breathed. So I was at home.

"Nothing," I wanted to say, but my voice didn't come out. "She fell," explained Fat Gwenven, who held me. She laid me on the bed. I sat up immediately, feeling slightly bewildered as to what was going on. My body was wide awake, but my mind was tired.

"Your mother has gone to fetch the Wise One," said Gwenven, "before they get here, you just have time to take off your dirty clothes and have a wash. There's just enough fresh water in the tub." The water was cold, but the hearth fire was hot. I was grateful that I didn't have to go to the well and lucky that I had fallen on soft muddy grass instead of into a thorny hedge. I was not hurt, not even bruised or scratched – no-one could understand why I had passed out. I told the old priestess everything, when she arrived.

"The men of iron scared me," I said, "although I knew they weren't really there. The blade of grass was like a sword and I thought I fell a hundred paces into a hole…"

"Frightened little doe," said the wise woman, "you know nearly as much as I. The Men of Iron will come and we must be prepared to defend ourselves. There are troubled times ahead and every blade of grass will be precious to us. The men of iron will bring a sickness to our land. There will be sores on the land, which will take many generations to heal, after so much ravaging and pillaging. The Green Folk will retreat further from our world, as they cannot endure the black metal. It will be hard to grow food. Then every little bit will matter, every blade of grass."

It took me many years to fully understand what she meant. Was it the Queen of the Green Folk who caught me in her soft arms, or simply a fat servant woman? I may never know. Even the old wise one had difficulties understanding how I could have fallen senseless without being hurt and finally came round bright-eyed and wide awake. Some mysteries were impossible for humans to work out. However, the vision of the men of iron had to be taken notice of. Those of us with the sight were forbidden to fight with earthly weapons and I never wanted to play battles again.

Extract from: "Land of the Setting Sun" (Historical Novel)

11

Crossed Wires

Crossed Wires

Eileen sat on the sofa, twiddling with her hair, alternately biting her nails. The doorbell rang and she heard a familiar voice shout:

"Can I come in?" She got up and opened the door. She hadn't wanted to see Paul, not after what he had told her last week.

"What do you want?" she said.

"What's up?" he replied, as if nothing had happened.

"You know bloody well," said Eileen.

"Ah, put the kettle on."

"Put it on yourself, you know where it is." Eileen was still so cross and upset, now totally perplexed at Paul's behaviour. They sat at the kitchen table. She poured the coffee without speaking. He lit a cigarette and she placed the ashtray on the table.

"She's got the hump since I met her yesterday."

So, she looks even worse now than she does anyway, thought Eileen. How will I ever know when he's telling me the truth now, after all those lies?

How can he even still say 'hello' to her, after all she had done to him? I would take out an injunction on her, if I were him.

"Thanks," said Eileen, without looking up, when he handed her a bar of chocolate.

"You're very quiet," he said, "someone upset you?" Eileen got up and picked up the small mirror from the hallway and held it in front of Paul. He frowned, then he laughed. His phone rang and he answered:

"Hello." He frowned.

"What do you mean she's at the station? What's she done?"

Eileen smiled.

12

Water Water

Water! Water!

One last gurgle and that old washing machine finally gave up the ghost. George, from a few houses away fitted the new one free of charge and frowned at the weird plumbing. Everyone had said the same and I had thought so, too and knew I'd have to get it re-organised some day, but at the moment I was skint after getting a new carpet for the hallway and then a new washing machine. George was a handyman, not a plumber.

"It wasn't me who put in those pipes," he said emphatically, "it was some adventurer who didn't have a clue." In my delightfully large kitchen the washing machine was 8ft away from the sink with unsightly pipes halfway across the room running along the worktops. George and I both watched the trial wash and spin, never once looking at those pipes. I was most pleased with my new mean machine and George was happy with the bottle of homemade blackberry wine as payment for his efforts.

I went about my business, hung up the washing and cleaned the worktops. I wiped a little puddle on top of the fridge, then fixed the damp patch on the pipe with insulation tape. I loaded another wash, so Brian, my lodger would have some clean clothes for work tomorrow. I was dusting the sitting room when I heard a loud wail. Freddy, the cat came walking along the hallway leaving wet prints on the new carpet.

"Oh my God!" I dropped the duster and ran into the kitchen. At first I could see nothing except for cat paw prints on the freshly wiped worktops. The kitchen sink was full and bubbling like a boiling kettle. There was nothing noticeable under the sink. There must be a blockage somewhere, I'll have to get George back.

I switched off the machine and watched the load going in slow motion and grinding to a halt. The water drained down the plug hole with a rumble and left a dirty rim around the sink. Every few seconds it spluttered back up. I put in the plug and all was quiet. There was no answer when I knocked on George's door, so I returned home. All was well. I must have done the right thing with the plug and decided to finish the wash. When it began to spin the pipes began to rattle, but remained dry. Then without warning a dirty fountain came up straight from the sink and sent the plug flying across the room. I switched off the machine and pulled out the mains. More dirty water came spluttering out and now there was a leak under the sink with one of the taps dripping. I placed a large saucepan under it to catch the drops. The duct tape refused to stick to the wet tap, which began dripping more profusely now. I will have to call a plumber!

I pulled out the Yellow Pages from the cupboard, then dialled a number to get an answering machine with an annoying female voice:

"All our plumbers are busy at the moment. If you wish to make an appointment, please leave a message with your name and address. In an emergency please call 089...." I called the emergency number, which was answered by a monotonous female voice. I explained the situation. The girl said:

"All our plumbers are out on call at the moment, but we will get someone to contact you as soon as possible." Five minutes later the saucepan under the sink was full and my stress levels were rising in line with the water. The drips were becoming more frequent. I'll have to phone them again.

"Can you turn off the stop cock?" The girl asked me.

"Where's that?"

"Under the sink."

"That's where it's leaking. Which way do I turn it?"

"To the left." I tried, it didn't move, maybe it takes someone stronger than me. Typically, there was no-one here to help when needed. When I managed to turn the stop cock, it wasn't dripping anymore – it was streaming! I screamed. The thing resisted me when trying to turn it the other way. I could feel the force of the stream. Then Plop! The pipe over the other side, nearest the washing machine had come unhinged and more water came gushing out. I went for the mop and bucket. There was no stopping the flood now. I dialled the emergency number again.

"You will have to switch it off at the water point."

"What? Where's that?"

"Out in the street, by the front door." I had no idea what she was talking about.

"I have two bloody waterfalls in my kitchen!" I yelled down the phone. "I need a plumber Now!"

"All our plumbers are busy right now. We'll send someone out as soon as possible." I slammed down the phone and let out an expletive. I put on my wellies and went out to get help. Jim next door but one was a builder, but likely to be at work. I banged at his door, shouting: "Help!" Pat, his wife came to the rescue in her wellies and with a large bucket.

The water was 6 inches high when we got back. The brand new hall carpet was a sponge and the kitchen vinyl floating. Pat didn't know where the water point was either. I dialled the number one last time.

"I'm sorry, all our plumbers are out on call. We are very busy today…"

"The water is knee high," I screamed, "can you hear it? It's coming out of two ends!"

"I can hear something, we're doing our best to send someone over as soon as possible. Meanwhile you will have to switch off the water."

"We can't find where to switch it off. You need to send someone now!"

"We're doing our best…"

"Your best, my arse! Can you hear this?" Pat was syphening saucepans into buckets.

"Can you hear that, you stupid cow!"

"Someone will be with you in about half an hour." I rammed down the receiver. "Half an hour! The whole house will be drowned by then."

"Call the fire brigade," Pat suggested.

"Will they sort this kind of thing?"

"They should. This is a real emergency now."

The plumber finally arrived to a spectacle of uniformed firemen draining my kitchen with a large hose. The following day George and Jim moved the washing machine and fitted proper pipes.

Extract from "Woman Trouble" (autobiographical novel)

13

To Know God is to Love
Many Things

To Know God is to Love Many Things

Some people go to church every Sunday out of habit or tradition. I don't believe God wants you to go to church and mumble prayers without thought or meaning.

God is everywhere at once. He is in nature and animals and plants. You can feel his presence in the trees, the forests, the rivers, the sea. If you love and respect nature you will learn to understand the meaning of life.

God is love, while places of worship and the people therein more often cause friction and even war.

Of course not all is peaceful in nature, but if you can see the beauty in the storm and accept the destruction of the old season to make room for the new. Life is an eternal cycle – everything dies and is reborn, like the flowers and the leaves on trees.

Love the sunshine, respect the rain. The world is a work of art everyone is working on. Work with your heart and God will guide you.

14

Interesting People

Interesting People

My horoscope for the week said that I was going to meet new interesting people and may experience some unexpected events. Well, that's one way of putting it. On the previous Saturday I had got chatting to a Canadian man on the train, telling him (like I tell everyone) that I was looking for a house to rent in Kilkenny City. The following Friday I met him again in the library and he told me that he knew a woman who lived near the cathedral and had been talking about letting out her house.

"She's moving back to London," said Norman, the Canadian. "If you're free for half an hour now I'll take you to her and if she's in, you can talk about it." Off we went to the little row of houses by the cathedral and rang Nora's bell. A woman in a long skirt and cardigan, with dishevelled black hair opened the door and Norman introduced us. We sat down with a coffee in a very untidy front room. Nora chatted endlessly about her daughter's long holiday in Lanzarote, her sons and her two ex-husbands. To my disappointment Nora wasn't moving out at all and she was renting the house herself. She was thinking of sharing the house with someone, as her children had all left home. My hopes were shattered again. A while ago I had made a vow that I would never share a house with a woman again, as in my experience that had never worked out well. Men are much more easy-going. Apart from that, I need more space for all my stuff.

Women are like cats, quarrelling over territory. Put

two female strangers into a room for a weekend and there will be sparks flying. Put two female friends into a room for the same time and they are guaranteed to become enemies.

"My youngest son is fifteen. He doesn't live here all the time, but stays here sometimes." Nora was London Irish with an accent similar to mine. "My older son broke both his legs."

"That's horrible. How did he do that?"

"My daughter was living in London with her father and she was really unhappy with her stepmother…" Nora went off on a totally different track and I asked the same question twice more before she finally told me:

"He slipped on this floor here." It was rather difficult to have a conversation with her, as she never answered a question, but trailed off into a different direction beginning to tell a story which had nothing to do with the question.

"I could do with someone to tidy this place up," Nora continued. "I'm really useless at cleaning." Judging by the state of the room, she was being very honest.

"I'm quite good at housework, I think. I couldn't live here with teenagers going in and out the house and there would be no room for all my stuff, but I'm happy to do some cleaning for you."

"Would you? That would be great. When?"

"Tomorrow afternoon, if you like. About three?"

"That's brilliant. Is twelve euros an hour o.k.?"

"Yes, sure. See you tomorrow." Still no house, but

I have got a job here, maybe even a regular arrangement. Things are looking up.

When I arrived at the house the next day at the said time, the front room was in a worse mess than the day before. There was broken glass on the floor, a shattered ceramic sugar bowl with sugar all over the place. Cushions, shoes, socks, cigarette butts, beer-stained family photographs, drops of red wine, pens and newspapers strewn around the floor. Perhaps this was meant to be a peculiar work of art by someone like Tracy Emin, I wondered. A man sat on the sofa, smoking.

"That's Rob," Nora introduced him. "He's my boyfriend." Rob screwed up his face suggesting that he was not in a relationship with Nora, except perhaps on a very part-time basis. Nora, who still looked like an unmade bed with her hair resembling a raided crows nest, apologised for the state of her house.

"Sorry about this mess. I had some people round last night."

"That's no problem. It won't take me long to clean it up."

"It'll take hours," said Rob. "Nobody should be expected to clean that sort of mess up."

"I'll do it. I'm sure it looks worse than it is. If you want me to do the whole house, it'll take about three hours or so." Nora was barefoot and her feet had been through the wars – the red drops weren't wine! When she left the room to go to the bathroom, Rob handed me a fifty Euro note and asked:

"Will that do for now?"

"Yes, sure, thank you very much." I started in the kitchen washing up a large pile of dirty dishes and tidying away food stuff. It must have been quite some party! Rob came up to me and put another tenner into my pocket and commented:

"You should be getting paid lots more for this sort of work." I couldn't believe my luck. If this was going to be a regular job I would be doing well. Rob left the house, telling me that he was coming back later to chat to me about some other jobs he may have for me. Nora went upstairs to bed and I carried on cleaning. After sweeping up and binning the whole mess on the front room floor I set to work with the hoover. When Nora returned from her catnap, it was all done.

"That's wonderful!" She exclaimed. "You have done a wonderful job."

"Do you want me to do upstairs?"

"You can change the beds if you want. I've bought new sheets and covers."

"O.k. Can I have a cup of coffee, please? I'm really thirsty."

"Of course you can."

"Do you want one?"

"No thanks." At that moment Rob returned, praising me for my efforts and handed me another tenner.

"I have got a couple of houses I'm selling in Bagnelstown," he told me, "and once they're ready they will need cleaning. This could be two or three days work and you'll get your petrol paid for and your meals."

"That sounds fun. Can I get a bus to Bagnelstown and back?" He didn't know.

"What sort of cleaning can you do?" This seemed a strange question.

"Tell me what you want done and I'll tell you if I can do it."

"Polishing skirting boards?"

"No problem."

"Can you put up curtain rails?"

"No, sorry, I couldn't do that. But I might know someone who can. I've a friend who does all sorts of jobs like that and he has a car as well." We chatted for a while and then Nora said pointing at Rob:

"This man has got a lot of houses." I had gathered from our conversation that Rob must be some sort of property developer.

"You wouldn't have one in the city?" I enquired, hopefully.

"Yes, actually there is one just off John Street that I want to rent out." Apparently, the house was just being done up, fully insulated with gas central heating, a bath, garden in the front and the back. The furniture could be moved around and there should be room for more if I needed it – I probably will! It sounded too good to be true.

"Two single bedrooms." This seemed odd, since houses are often let out to couples who would want a double bed. I will want a double bed, as I'm not going to retire from life. I would have to see the house. Rob said it would be ready for viewing on Wednesday and gave me his phone number scribbled on a piece of paper. Nora did not want me to polish the floor nor put the rug back where it used to be.

"My son slipped on this floor and broke both his legs. I think I'm going to put sand on it to make it safe." Rob shook his head.

"You can't put sand on a wooden floor!" Maybe I should have left the sugar there. I asked Nora if she wanted me to do the beds and hoover upstairs. Rob said I could do it another time, as the couple clearly had other things in mind, which didn't require my presence. I went home happy.

On the Monday night I went to see Joe and amongst other things, asked him if he could put up curtain rails.

"Yes, sure, any sort of jobs like that." I told him what had happened over the weekend and all the money I had made for a bit of cleaning.

"I need someone to drive me there and back and he might have some work for you as well. He'll pay for the petrol, food we need and of course for the work."

"That sounds good. If the weather isn't too bad, we can take our time on the way back and I'll show you some nice places."

"That would be great. I'm going to look at a house in the city on Wednesday, too – fingers crossed! I don't want to tempt fate though by talking about it just yet. I want to see it first." However, Joe agreed that the work opportunity seemed genuine and we both looked forward to being a team for a couple of days.

I dialled the number Rob had given me on Tuesday night and got through to a woman's voice on an answering machine. Maybe it's an office number. I'll try again tomorrow. I got the same answering machine again and left a message for Rob. My hopes began to fade when Nora didn't answer her phone either. So I decided to go to her home and see if she had any details about the house or at least knew where I could find Rob.

Nora's front door was wide open and as I approached it, a man staggered out with his hands and face covered in blood. Next door a couple of builders were painting the outside walls of the house. Without getting too close I asked the blood-faced man if he was alright.

"Yeah," he said. From his manner and the smell of his breath I could tell that he was very drunk. He must have cut himself on a broken bottle or something.

"What have you done to your hands and face?"

"Blood brothers," he hiccupped. "I'm an Irish Celt. That's what we do. You wouldn't know…" I jumped backward, as he held a bloody hand up to me as if he wanted me to taste it.

Yes, I do know! The whole thing would have been even weirder and scarier if I had not heard of this ancient practice. For my interest in ancient history I had read about these blood rituals on several occasions. When a warrior was injured in battle, his friend would take a little blood from a fresh wound and wash his face with it. This would bond the two warriors in a strong friendship and give them further courage and strength to go into battle again. The wife or lover of a mortally wounded warrior would take a drop of blood to her lips to have a part of her beloved to keep forever. Our drunk, of course, had twisted the whole tradition by wiping the blood from his own hands all over his face. Or had he?

"Is Nora in?" I asked.

"Yeah, she's upstairs in bed." He went back inside and yelled her name. There was no reply. He told me I could go upstairs and talk to her, but I wasn't going to take chances. He managed to stumble halfway up the stairs, shouting:

"Nora! Someone down here to see ya!" No reply. The decorators next door had been watching us and one of them came over to suggest:

"If we keep him busy and don't let him in the house, would you go upstairs and see if the woman is alright. I don't like the look of all this." I agreed and went upstairs with mixed feelings as to what I was going to find. It crossed my mind that the drunk might have carved her up in her bed and it was her blood on his hands and face.

The first bedroom was a shocking mess with sheets and duvets piled up on the bed and clothes on the floor. The second and third were in much the same state until the pile of duvets on the double bed stirred and a bedraggled Nora looked up at me.

"Are you alright?" I enquired, relieved to see no

blood anywhere.

"I don't know. I haven't been raped, have I? I don't think I've been raped." Surely any woman who had been raped would remember it, even if she had been drunk at the time.

"I think I have been drugged."

"Do you want me to call the guards?"

"I don't feel right. I think I've been drugged."

"Who's that man with blood on his face? Do you know him?"

"Not very well."

"Do you need any help? I think I'll call the guards. You'll be o.k. now." I told the builders that Nora was alive and what she had said about having been drugged. One of them called the guards, who arrived within ten minutes. One officer went upstairs to speak to Nora and the other asked me to wait while he questioned the aspiring Celtic warrior. I heard the drunk say:

"This is Rob's house." Then he told him about the blood ritual. The Garda wrote down my name and address and I told him what I had seen and why I was there. His colleague returned and asked me if I was related to Nora. Obviously the accent seemed to suggest that.

"No, I hardly know her."

"Does she have a drink problem herself?"

"I don't know, but she seems to have some sort of problem."

"Who owns that house?"

"No idea. The builders might know." They spoke

to the decorators for a couple of minutes, during which time the blood-faced drunk staggered back into the house and fell over. The Gardai picked him up and he didn't resist as they bundled him into the car.

Only a moment later my mobile rang. It was the woman from the answering machine and when I said that I was trying to get hold of Rob, she replied:

"He is not here. I haven't seen him in four months."

"Four months? I thought you worked for him."

"I do. I answer the phone. This is a good number to have given you." What is she talking about? How many numbers does he have?

"What do you do? Are you his secretary?"

"I can't tell you that. I don't know you." The plot thickens.

"He said he had a house in Kilkenny I could look at today, because I'm looking for a house to rent. He also said he might have some cleaning work for me." I could picture the woman frowning at the other end of the phone, as she didn't have a clue what I was getting at.

"Does he do up houses for sale and for rent?" I continued. "Is that his business?"

"I can't tell you what he does. Sorry." I thanked her for calling me back.

"If I hear from Rob I will pass on your message." I expect never to hear from Rob or Nora or anyone of them again and who Rob (if that's his real name) is will forever remain a mystery. He may be a drug dealer or a pimp or simply a property developer fiddling his taxes.

I was disappointed to have been conned again, when I realised that there probably was no house off John Street, no jobs in Bagnelstown or anywhere else and this may be just as well. It was best not to get involved in any dodgy business. Next time my horoscope mentions meeting interesting people I shall be prepared for any possibility and then no events could be totally unexpected.

15

Earth

Earth

Twenty years ago Michael Murphy had come to this same pub, which then was buzzing. People of all ages came in, some with musical instruments would start playing and singing a mix of traditional and modern. Everybody talked to everybody else, sharing ideas, telling jokes and enjoying life. Now they individually retreated into corners with laptops and smart phones and didn't know their neighbours' names, let alone speak to strangers.

Now Michael Murphy sat at the bar, reminiscing, making one pint of Guinness last an hour, so he could drive home safely before dark. He wished he hadn't come here now. This place was too full of memories. If he hadn't come here twenty years ago, he wouldn't have met her, got married, bought a house worth three times his income, got divorced, unemployed and lost it all, then ended up sharing a small over furnished flat with a 22-year-old college student. He came down here to clear his head, when to the contrary the place depressed him.

I should have gone to the woods or that nice pond with the swans. The white haired old woman by the window, who had been watching him, got up and called:

"Good bye, God bless!"

"Bye," replied the landlord from behind the bar. Michael went to hold the door for her.

"Thank you," she said and smiled at him. "You will be blessed." He frowned and noticed how very old she was. She had long white hair and a million wrinkles, and striking green eyes full of knowledge as well as youthful innocence.

"She is in here nearly every day in that same place just watching people," the publican told Michael, "never buys anything." Michael shrugged. On his way out, he saw a shiny object on the table where the old woman had sat, and picked it up. It was a beautiful gold bracelet with intricate Celtic designs. There was no hallmark on it, though he could tell it was real gold by the feel and the weight of it. Michael didn't trust anyone in the pub and decided to give the bracelet back to the old woman in person. She can't have gone far. He got into his car and drove down the lane towards the village – so he thought. He remembered the houses weren't too far from the ancient burial mound and the standing stone, he had just passed. Right ahead the earth was freshly dug and piled up like a giant mole hill.

They must have found another Neolithic site. Looks nothing special though. He drove on. There were no road signs anywhere and the lane came to an abrupt end by a hedge of hawthorns. Michael got out of the car and peered over the hedge. There was a large trench on the other side, which looked fairly new.

"Oh shit!" Michael tripped over a stone and fell down a hole. It was a deep and dark hole. He fumbled for his phone and swore again, when he could get no signal. All he could do was to try and push and lift himself up somehow, except that the earth was soft and mossy around him and the stones were loose. The silence unnerved him. He tried his phone again to no avail and as he held it, he dropped the gold bracelet.

"Bugger!" He picked up a pebble and threw it to the ground in anger. More stones fell, one hit his foot.

I have to get out of here! The earth crumbled, stones cracked like a minor earthquake. A woman's voice called his name.

"Michael! Michael Murphy!"

"Who's there?" There was no reply. It was easier to move now. Michael pushed the earth up like a mole, and just like a mole he managed to pull himself up to the surface. He felt shaken up and fairly bewildered and would have to gather himself before going back to the car. He made it to the other side of the hawthorn hedge, where the white haired old woman stood smiling at him. He stared. She was wearing the gold bracelet on her wrist.

"Who are you?" She did not answer. Instead she said:

"Thank you for bringing it back. You are blessed."

Michael Murphy's life changed completely. He discovered talents he didn't know he had, with a compulsion to work with the earth. He made sculptures and statues with great care and detail. They became so popular that he managed to make a living from what started as a hobby. After a couple of years he bought a little townhouse and got the garden thriving within weeks. When asked in an interview with a local newspaper what inspired him to create such beautiful works of art, he replied: "The Earth."

16

George Clooney is Coming to Kilkenny

George Clooney is Coming to Kilkenny

Mary sits outside a cafe with a cappucino and a cigarette, reading the last chapter of a thriller. Alison walks up to her and calls out:

"What are you reading?" Alison tries to get a glance at the title of Mary's thriller. Mary holds up the book.

"Is this any good?"

"Great! Can't put it down. Another five pages. I think they leave it to the last page before you know who did it and it's always someone you least expect it to be."

"I wouldn't have the patience. It would have me tormented. I'll have to read the last page before the last chapter." Mary shakes her head. Alison isn't into books like Mary. She is into films and television.

"I got exciting news!" she says. Mary stubs out her cigarette into the ashtray and looks up at her friend.

"Well, sit down and have a coffee."

"Have you heard?"

"What?"

"George Clooney is coming to Kilkenny! This time he really is, you know, it was on the news and all."

"I believe it when I see it." Mary shrugs. True, George Clooney had given everyone false hope so many times before. Since then, he'd gone and got married. So why would he still be of so much interest to anyone? However, Alison is full of enthusiasm.

"You better make sure you got batteries in your camera."

"Do you really think he's going to pose for you?" Mary is just a bit annoyed at the interruption. She had got so engrossed in that thriller.

"I've got the money saved for the hairdresser and the beauty treatment, complete make-over, sunbed and then getting my nails done, fingers and toes."

"Jesus, Alison, he's coming here to see his ancestral home, he's hardly gonna look at your toes."

"I've also got the dress," Alison goes on, "got it in a charity shop, but no-one needs to know that. An incentive to lose a couple of stone."

"George Clooney is a married man now," Mary reminds her friend.

"I wonder what she'll be wearing. You know, what's her name?"

"Mrs. Clooney," grumps Mary. "Something very classy, I'd think."

"She can afford it, but what are you going to wear?"

Mary shrugs, and thinks. Something that won't upstage you, Alison. More important to make sure the town's tidy, the streets are clean and the flowers are watered... She tries to read again. Four and a half pages, ten to fifteen minutes, and she would know who did it. But Alison pulls out a chair and sits opposite, calls the waitress and orders a black coffee. Mary's face is back in the book.

"Is it really that good?" Alison interrupts again.

"Yes, it's brilliant, another four pages..."

"Would it make a good movie?"

"Sure, it's a better story than any movie I've seen with George Clooney in it."

Alison makes a face.

"Do you think he'll be filming while he's in Kilkenny? Wouldn't that be great?"

"Yeah, wouldn't be bad." Mary says monotonously without looking up. The waitress arrives with Alison's coffee.

"You know George Clooney is coming to Kilkenny?" Alison turns to the waitress.

"Oh, George Calooney," she says enthusiastically, "I love George Calooney." Never mind the Lithuanian mis-pronunciation, Alison is over the moon to have found a kindred spirit, and Mary gets to the end of her thriller. She closes the book and lights another cigarette, as the waitress moves on to take an order from another table.

"When is he coming then?" asks Mary.

"Don't know yet," says Alison, "but he definitely is."

17

The Gift of Memory

The Gift of Memory

I was born in 2057, just barely a year after my death. I have the gift of memory. The world had already gone strange and dangerous in the 2020's and it is a big surprise that the human race is still in existence now in 2084.

I am afraid to have children, knowing they may not live to grow up. I am one of the last few left with the memory of a free world. My life is in danger. World War III has been postponed twice, as our invaders want to see everyone suffer before they push the nuclear button and blow the whole planet to smithereens.

I was married twice to the same man. Once in our old tradition which had to remain secret, then in a public show pretending we belonged to them. But they found out who we were and now imprisoned us. I am in a female jail and my husband is a million miles away in a men's. Telepathy comes with the gift of memory. So we communicate through our thoughts and our dreams.

"Don't panic," he tells me, "don't give them what they want. I'm far away, but I'm always with you. Don't give up!" The only comfort I have in my cold dark cell is the closeness of a loving soul. The memory gives strength of spirit and faith.

Love is an outdated emotion, supposed to be discouraged in the same way as lust, and never allowed to be publicly demonstrated. My husband and I fell in love, so we got married and for a short while we were left in peace. My brother did not have the gift of memory. He was lost and rootless and confused. He certainly did not belong to the tyrants, but he did not find a strong connection with us either. While he did not have the memory that my husband and I were born with, my brother had high emotions carried over from a distant past. It was hard for him to keep his love a secret. My brother and his lover were brought to court and executed, simply for showing love for each other.

No-one can be trusted, when lying and deceiving is taught to five-year-olds in schools. I remember beautiful clothes and fun music and dancing, and walking dogs in the woods in my previous life.

Dogs are extinct now, since the oppressors killed each and every one of them. Trees are becoming rare. Everywhere there is desert sand or muddy pampas. Food is mass produced in intensive factory farms.

We have no books, no internet to learn of the old ways. They have taken everything which offends them. The only thing remaining is our memory. Now they are working on a device to take that away, too.

18

Look What the Cat Brought In

Look What the Cat Brought In

A lovely sunny day, when clouds began to gather. I looked at the sky and decided to bring in the nearly dry washing, just in case. As I stepped into the garden, a tiny bright blue feather tumbled down at my feet. This couldn't be from a native bird.

A loud scream sent my dog running next door, barking.

Maureen has fallen off her deckchair, was my first thought.

"Help!"

"Are you alright, Maureen? What's up?"

"Come here, come here, quick!" Her voice was panicky. "Look what your cat brought into my house!" Recently my cat Oscar had been spending more time next door than in his own home. Of course it was Maureen's fault for feeding him treats.

"Can you come in please?" My neighbour urged me.

"Can you try and rescue the poor thing. Don't let Oscar run out with it."

"Rescue it?" She screamed. "I'm not going to touch it!"

"I'll be there in a sec." Luckily the front door was open. Maureen stood on top of a chair in the hallway, trembling.

"Where is the little devil?" I asked.

"In the kitchen. I'm not going in there, you can't make me!"

It must be a budgie escaped from somewhere in the neighbourhood. What is she making such a fuss about?

"I hope the bird isn't hurt." Then I opened the kitchen door and saw Oscar swishing his tail staring at a huge rat by the door to the yard. I got my dog Ruby to chase it out into the bushes outside the gate. She barked up the tree where a little blue bird flew away, leaving me another little feather. Oscar moved back home, as he was never allowed in next door again.

19

No Room at the Inn

No Room at the Inn

They had timed it well, to evict their tenants just before Christmas, the season of goodwill. Landlords are a charitable lot. They go out shaking buckets for the homeless, but don't look at their own backyards – hypocrites!

Mary and Joseph had only got married a month ago, and then Joe, as a self-employed carpenter had been unable to get enough work to pay the rent and couldn't get help from the state. They sold some of their wedding presents, but it didn't get them too far. They slept in their van, which wasn't ideal, but better than the street.

"I'm pregnant," Mary announced to her husband, who was too depressed to react joyfully.

"I hope we're going to find a half decent place to live before the baby is born," he said.

"I don't know," Mary didn't seem worried, "he's due any day now."

"What?" It was hard to believe, as Mary didn't show any signs of pregnancy.

"Gabriel told me, our son will be born at Christmas and he'll be a very special child."

"Gabriel who?" Joe frowned.

"The Angel Gabriel," said Mary and Joseph looked relieved.

"We'd better find somewhere to stay immediately." Joe started the van and drove out along a country lane. They stopped at a petrol station. He paid for the petrol and saw a sign for 'Rooms to Let'.

"Sorry, there's no room here," they were told, "we're booked from tonight." They came to a few more B & B's, who rejected them. Then on Christmas Eve the van broke down, just when it was getting dark.

"We won't get anyone to fix it now." Joseph took a bag of necessities, then locked the doors.

"Are you ok walking?"

"Sure, I'm fine." It began to snow.

"That's all we need," Joe grumbled.

"Oh, it's so beautiful!" Mary was truly captivated, catching the dancing snowflakes in her hands.

"The ambulances should be working, maybe they'll get you to the hospital," said Joe. He took his phone from his coat pocket, but found the battery had gone flat.

"We have to go back to the van," Joe insisted, "at least we'll be dry." Mary pointed at a farm an equal distance away. When Joseph saw a small bright light in the hedge rows moving towards them, he was sure they were both losing their minds. At first his wife was convinced that she was nine months pregnant, because an angel told her so in a dream. Then she was playing with snowflakes and refusing to go to hospital. Now he was hallucinating, seeing shooting stars in a hedge.

It's the stress, he told himself, being evicted, rejected and having to spend Christmas out in the cold would do anybody's head in.

A rustle in the hedge and the light jumped, almost blinding Joe for a second. Right before them was a sheep dog with an illuminated collar. Mary smiled and Joe sighed with relief. The dog turned and walked slowly along the path, looking back occasionally to make sure the couple was following.

The stable door was ajar and the dog slipped in. It was a big stable with two horses settled for the night on straw. A tabby cat was curled up sleeping on top of a beam, in the corner. The only light was that attached to the dog's collar. It was warm and dry. Mary sat on a bale of straw with the sheep dog at her feet. Joseph sat opposite his wife, trying to make sense of the calm, radiant expression on her face. She must be tired, like he was.

Time passed and they listened to distant church bells and later the sound of a car in the driveway, shining in a temporary light. The dog got up and ran into the yard greeting the people home from Midnight Mass. Mary stood up in the darkness and announced:

"The baby is coming!" Until this moment the ever realistic and practical Joseph had believed the baby was a figment of Mary's imagination, but all that screaming and shouting and squirming in pain could not be acting. If only he could see... He had to go and get help. As soon as he found his way to the stable door, the dog ran towards him with a young woman holding a torch.

"Can you help?" Joe asked desperately. "My wife is having a baby right now!" The woman helped Mary into a position and put the torch down, talking soothingly.

"My name is Carol," she said, "it's my birthday today." Mary tried to say 'Happy Birthday' but her voice turned into a wail. Carol delivered the baby boy with expertise, then handed him to his mother.

"I have helped a lot of lambs into the world," explained Carol as a matter of fact, " and a couple of foals." She patted the dog.

"Good girl, Star." The horses stood and observed, without a sound. The cat sat undisturbed on the beam with paws tucked in and watched, as the stable filled with light. After the first meal of his mother's milk, the baby was wrapped in Mary's scarf and laid into a crib with clean straw. Carol creaked the stable door, which refused to close.

"I'll fix that for you," Joseph suggested.

The following day, Carol returned with a cooked breakfast and soft blankets. Outside the snow had settled picturesquely. Carol fed the horses and decided to leave the sheep in the pen for now. Her parents came to say 'hello' and none of them felt the event was strange. Carol's mother believed in miracles, when this day, 21 years ago she had given birth to a healthy baby girl, when nobody had even known she was expecting. The weather had been even worse that night with blizzards preventing them from attending church. The contented mother was feeding her newborn, while listening to the Christmas carol concert on the radio, and thus decided her daughter's name.

Mary was warm and comfortable in the stable and had no desire to move into the farm house, or even join Carol and her parents for Christmas Dinner.

While the family was busy preparing and eating the big dinner, they didn't notice an old vintage car driving into the yard. Star, the dog greeted the driver and led him to the stable.

"Caspar," said Mary and smiled at the small built man, who resembled a chieftain of ancient Ireland with long red hair and moustaches, wearing a brown coat and green trousers. He placed a carved and polished wooden box by the crib and opened it. Joseph examined the intricate Celtic designs of the carvings and Mary looked at the contents. Incense and scented candles. Caspar said he had made all this himself as a special gift for the child, and the box was made from the wood of twenty-seven different trees.

Another day passed, when Star brought another visitor. In spite of his exotic appearance, he had slipped into the stable unseen by anyone in the farm house. Melchior was an oriental, dressed in saffron robes. He brought the gift of myrrh contained in a porcellain jar beautifully painted in Chinese symbols.

In the following days, more visitors came and went – farmers and shopkeepers from surrounding areas. Some came out of pure curiosity and many left presents for the baby. Awe struck by the pure white light above the heads of the child and his mother, all left in an upbeat mood, even those who had arrived in a down one. Even the local drunk was allowed to see in the New Year in the pub, keeping his promise to not cause a disruption. No more than slightly tipsy he would entertain the customers with stories of what he had seen just a few days ago.

Finally Balthasar arrived with a heavy case filled with pure gold coins. He explained his delay with "Customs didn't believe that ten pounds of gold was a gift for a child. They questioned me for hours, over and over again, even put me on a lie detector." He had claimed that he had followed the instructions of God to collect the coins, until a message from the Angel Gabriel told him what to do next. Caspar laughed.

"At least I didn't have to travel too far. Frankincense could have been mistaken for illegal drugs at any airport." Melchior, easily recognised as an oriental holy man, had encountered no problems, as no-one had even checked the contents of the painted jar. Balthasar was conspicuous with his dreadlocks and rainbow coloured African shirt.

At the farm and its surroundings nobody asked questions, no journalists came to the stable. One young enthusiast had thought of taking pictures on his smart phone, but was convinced that no-one would believe him, if he posted them on social media. Everyone would think they were staged and photoshopped. But he had seen the light around the baby and it was real, and out of respect he would not take snaps. The landlady of the B & B, who had lied when she told Mary and Joseph that she had no vacancies, was hugely embarrassed and hoped they would not recognise her when she quietly placed a 50 euro note under the crib.

Eventually the snow melted and the three wise men bid farewell and returned each to their home in three different continents.

Word got out, after Joe repaired the stable door as promised. The van was running again and his phone never stopped ringing with job offers. Everything began to fall into place.

Rumours spread around the country and beyond. A baby had been born to a homeless couple in a stable, as no-one had offered them shelter. The child was given a lot of precious and unusual presents and had three most interesting visitors from three different continents. Many listened to the story, then shrugged and went about their daily business. The daily struggles of others did not concern them, when they had always taken their own home, car, holidays and all the latest gadgets simply for granted. Some would continue to milk the system, as they had always done and use the misfortunes of others to their advantage. Those who had experienced hardship, however, may read in this story a message of new hope. How many more times would history have to repeat itself until humans would finally wake up and see? God has given a second chance, perhaps the last opportunity for people to stop greed, turn hate into peace, indifference into compassion and make the world a better place.

20

Off The Rails

Off The Rails

It was the strangest sort of robbery. The clothes were taken off the rails and scattered all over the floor – none of them missing.

The shop resembled a battle field, without the blood. The sales assistants were busy tidying up, folding clothes, filling shelves. The rails stood upright, empty like skeletons over one side. The manager opened the cash register and started counting.

"It's all still there," she frowned. "I don't know how to report this." All the clothes hangers had been stolen. Cheap plastic clothes hangers!

21

She Said It Was an Accident – Was It Really?

She Said It Was an Accident – Was It Really?

We were all praying for him to wake up. I was sure I saw his eyes flicker for a split second. I told the nurse who then checked his heartbeat.

"It'll take time," she said, "he's through the worst, he'll be ok." I was instructed to return to the waiting room, a place which had become my second home lately. I slipped through the other door into the hospital garden. I needed fresh air, especially after seeing *her* sit there darkening the corner, staring at the floor. She told everyone it was an accident. Oh, but was it really? She was the one driving and came out totally unharmed. This wasn't the first time he ended up in intensive care because of her. Things are supposed to come in threes, so hopefully this was the last. Food poisoning – bad fish, put down to river pollution. Then there was this obscure virus that put him into isolation for over a week. Five doctors they employed to analyse it and no-one could put a name on it. Whenever the medical profession doesn't quite know what something is, it's a virus! Oh and now this car accident! The insurance will pay for what once was a ten-year-old car in perfect working order. If he doesn't fully recover, they will pay a good lot more to her, enough to buy a brand new car. But the nurse just told me he will be well, so thank God for that. Have they told her? Is that why she looks cross, because she didn't get her way? Accident! Ha…! Karma will be the judge of that! Just you wait!

22

Pond Life

Pond Life

Leap Day! What's that supposed to mean? Why would anyone celebrate that, unless it happens to be your birthday. Or you are lucky enough to have a long term boyfriend to propose to. They had cards in the shops with 'Happy Leap Day!' Just another excuse to cash in on something. My friend Sharon put one through my letterbox with a picture of a big leaping frog. All my friends knew about my fascination with frogs, that goes back to my favourite fairytale 'The Princess and the Frog'. After one failed marriage, some would give up and settle for a single existence. After two divorces I was still hoping to get third time lucky. Knowing my luck, the frog I kiss probably turns into a princess. What would I do with that? There was the cliche of 'the prince turning up when you least expect it'. I always did find something I'd been looking for, when I started looking for something else. Right then, I needed a lodger more than a boyfriend, someone to help pay the bills.

"Not like you, not wanting to go out," said Elaine, "you're always up for a good knees-up." I shrugged.

"We can go out next week, I just don't want to go out for Leap Day."

"Ah go on," said Sharon in true Mrs. Doyle style, "I'll buy you a drink." So they persuaded me. I had nothing to lose.

I hadn't told anyone about the pond. I had discovered a clearing in the woods while walking my dog – a pond populated by frogs, newts and other small wildlife. It was a place like this where the princess met the frog that later became a prince.

The ground was still soggy after a heavy downpour, but something drew me to the pond. I had watched the frogs spawn a few days ago, the first sign of spring.

A heron stood guard on a small rock, scanning the pond for a potential meal. There were splashes in the water. I crouched down to see the frog spawn among the bog weed and budding marsh marigold. A pair of copper gold eyes stared up at me, then another, and another – too many to count. A whole tribe of frogs sat totally still holding my gaze. Just for fun I blew a kiss at a little frog, then got up and turned to leave. I heard a giggle and looked around to see a young girl stand by the pond.

"Hi," she said cheerfully.

"Hello," I returned. She was pretty, petite but curvy, if you could be that at the same time, with long shiny gold brown hair down her back. She wore a green coat and black boots.

"I love this place," she told me, "it's my birthday today and this is my favourite place to spend it."

"Happy Birthday!" I said, forgetting all about Leap Day. "Bye," I added and left, getting the feeling that I was somehow intruding. Perhaps she had arranged to meet someone there.

***

Sharon said she was looking for Mr. Right – we all are, Mr. Right or Mr. Perfect.
"I like to meet Mr. Riley," I said, only half joking. Sharon

laughed.

"What? Like O'Reillys pub? Maybe that's where we should go tonight."

"Yeah right, if you want to meet married men, farmers in their seventies," scowled Elaine, "singing drunk out of tune while eyeing you up."

"I said Riley, not O'Reilly. So that when we get married, we'll forever be living the Life of Riley." They could laugh, though I meant it.

As expected the nightclub was full of youngsters and the few older people there were in couples. The music was great, though – one lively dance after another. There, at the bar was the girl I had seen by the pond. She was wearing a floaty dress in greeny-blue chiffon and gold stiletto sandals. If anyone was going to pull tonight, sure it would have to be her.

"Hi," she said casually, "how's it going?"

"Not too bad, how are you?" A conversation wasn't too easy in a noisy nightclub.

"Grand," she said. "I'm Rana. Rana Marsh." I understood that she was here on her own, so I introduced her to Sharon and Elaine and we all ended up dancing together. Eventually it was quiet enough for us to talk better.

"I heard you're looking for a lodger," said Rana. Goodness, news travels fast in this town. Rumours spread like fire. I must have given her a really strange look, that made her giggle.

"Well, I'm looking for somewhere to stay," she

said. I didn't ask for references or proof of previous addresses, employers and all that. I only wanted to make sure she would get on with my cat and dog.

"Yes, sure. I love animals, wildlife, too, especially frogs." I needed to know nothing more. I couldn't have wished for a better lodger.

Her birthday was February 29th, which meant she only had had five birthdays at twenty years old. She was intelligent and mature, as well as fun-loving and outgoing. She was knowledgeable about many things and multi-talented. She had a lovely singing voice and was able to play a variety of musical instruments. She had a way with animals. She could design, paint, sew, cook, sing, dance, as well as being good at swimming, running, climbing trees and gymnastics.

Rana never spoke about her family or the place she grew up in. But I didn't want to pry. It didn't matter who her folks were. She was a decent and lovely young woman – like the daughter I never had. Daughters seem to be trouble in many people's lives. My ex-husband's daughter was largely to blame for our marriage breaking up. Sharon's daughter Melanie had been in Australia for nearly ten years with her boyfriend with no sign of wedding bells to give Sharon a chance to visit.

"I really hope I can see her walk down the aisle before she makes me a grandmother." I nodded, agreeing that would be the right order, and added:

"I'll make you a hat, as long as you let me know in time what colour dress you're wearing."

"Oh Jesus," Sharon sighed. "I could be wearing that hat for you sooner than for her." That wouldn't be a bad thing, though there was no sign yet of Mr. Riley. Elaine complained about her daughter preaching to her.

"Andrea tells me what to eat, what to wear, even what to say. She's going on and on about calories, additives and all that. Just about everything tasty is bad for you. It's like she's joined some weird religion. And have you seen her lately? Seen how skinny she's got? Because she doesn't eat anything and all those supplements are expensive. She says she's looking after her health, well I'm looking after my taste buds."

"Chocolate," I couldn't help adding, "no one tells me not to eat chocolate!"

"Quite right, and ice cream."

"And cake."

"Ah stop it, you're making me hungry." After all this, I believed it was a blessing not to be the mother of daughters. It saved me a lot of stress. Then I met Rana, the perfect daughter material.

That summer, prosperity flowed with ease. Rana and I were a team. We organised art exhibitions, fashion shows and charity events with overwhelming success, all thanks to Rana's marketing and PR skills. Stress didn't come into it, and excitement only in a good way.

I regularly went to clubs with my friends Sharon and Elaine. Sometimes Rana would join us, sometimes not. I had a date now and then, but it never came to more than a good night out.

"You're always the one who gets lucky lately." Sharon commented.

"It's only a date," I dismissed it.

"Isn't that how it starts, though," said Sharon, "chance would be a fine thing. I'm not even half as fussy as you."

"Maybe you should be more discerning. They were all very nice, but none of them was 'the one.'" Sharon rolled up her eyes.

"What if 'the one' never turns up?"

"I know he will!" I said emphatically. "I have everything else now – a foster daughter sort of, a steady income, success, fun, friendship, health, healthy animals, no stress."

"No stress!" Sharon didn't believe me.

***

Some people went to church on Sundays, some to the shopping centre. Rana and I went to the pond. Sometimes the frogs would come up and scrutinise me. Sure, they had their own idea of who I was. I did not walk my dog to the pond, during the months when the immediate area was alive with baby frogs that only recently had come on land. Rana climbed the large willow with ease and watched over the pond like a nature spirit. I was convinced I saw many more than her two eyes looking out of the trees reflecting in the water. Baby frogs and adults were swimming, some surfacing, sitting on small rocks statuesquely still. Most people would not even notice this place and walk past it. At first glance it was a water filled hole in the ground of no significance, not worth taking pictures of. Only a few of us understood that it was much much more. To our pagan ancestors it was a well of wisdom – a gateway between the mortal world and the Otherworld. The frogs were its guardians and the others were only seen, or even sensed by the spiritually sensitive.

Something wiggled in the water, something similar, but slimmer than a frog with a tail. A double-crested newt! A little pond animal on the register of protected endangered species face to face with me. He seemed to smile as I stared in awe. I gestured to Rana to come and see.

"Oh, you've seen a newt," she said as a matter of fact, "there's loads of them here."

"You're supposed to tell the Department of the Environment of any sightings of double-crested newts, so their numbers can be recorded." Rana shook her head vigorously and jumped out of the tree like a cat, landing on her feet.

"Recorded!" She spat the word and screwed up her face. "The reason why all the animals in and around this pond are thriving is because humans don't know of it. Bring people here with cameras and computers trampling all over it, wading through the pond in their wellies taking water samples, pulling out plants and demolishing habitat. That's why there are so many creatures threatened with extinction, because humans can't stop interfering with nature. Leave them in peace!" Never before had I heard

Rana raise her voice to speak with such passion and even an element of anger. However, I had to totally agree with her and was made to promise and swear never to tell anyone the location of the pond, not even my best friends.

Sharon and Elaine never shared my enthusiasm for pond life, so had no interest in searching for the pond or its inhabitants.

With Rana's permission I painted a picture of a double-crested newt. He was surrounded by marsh marigolds and a couple of frogs' faces peering out of the water. I showed my painting to my friends before putting it up for sale.

"Cute newt," said Sharon.

"He's smiling," Elaine noted rightly, "reminds me of my ex." Sharon laughed.

"He was a newt," she said, "of the inebriated variety." We all had to laugh at this clever piece of innuendo.

One of Rana's little eccentricities was that she loved the rain. Like most people I preferred the sun. A perfect evening was bright and warm after a sunny day. Rana felt compelled to go out into the garden when it was pouring. She enjoyed getting totally drenched. The rain refreshed and nourished her like a flower. It even brought the shine back to her hair. It had always done the opposite to me, making a right dog's dinner of my hair, turning it 80's style. I let the girl enjoy herself and watched her through the window while keeping safe and dry.

We organised a fashion show for the local cancer charity. Rana was a natural at organising as well as modelling. Mainly thanks to her, the show was a major success. It took a while to persuade Sharon and Elaine to take part.

"We don't want professional models, we want natural people of all ages, all shapes and sizes."

"I wouldn't want to parade all that fat in front of an audience," Elaine protested.

"Ah, go away," said Sharon, "you're only a sixteen."

"Does the whole world need to know my size?"

"I wish I had your boobs," said Sharon.

"Ah, would you listen to yourselves!" Rana couldn't stop laughing. "Just try some of those lovely clothes and see." Eventually she managed to convince them and they both thoroughly enjoyed it. Padded bras or control briefs – no-one needs to know what's underneath.

Rana never argued with anyone about anything. She saw the good in everything, or at least a silver lining. She did not believe in impossibilities. She had an ability to turn every challenge into an opportunity. She was also one of those enviable people who managed on only three or four hours of sleep, keeping healthy and full of energy. Until the beginning of October! Within a week she became tired and listless and was not the same girl who had brought so much fun and positive energy into my life during spring and summer. I had to let her sleep, she obviously needed the rest.

It is normal for the season, for me to become fatigued and at times irritable. I hate winter! The cold, the twenty hours of darkness in a day, the coughs and viruses spreading around, other people's down moods, not to mention the heating bills! I hate everything about winter and every year it comes around I wish I could hibernate through the whole duration of that season. Seasonal Affective Disorder! SAD! Rana must have a severe case of SAD! It could not be anything else. The poor girl became truly miserable. I tried to get medical advice.

"She's an adult, she needs to go to the doctor herself," was the answer.

"She's getting worse every day," I insisted, "she needs professional help." A pharmacist asked about her diet.

"That's the weird part," I said, "she's always hungry and put on about half a stone." The pharmacist explained it as:

"Comfort eating! It's a common symptom of any depressive illness."

So I spoke to Rana and tried to persuade her to see a doctor and be examined. She refused to take any sort of drugs and tried to convince me that she has these emotions every year.

"I know it'll pass. There will be another spring, it's nature!"

Oh God, I hope she won't be in this depression from October until March!

It hadn't been a great sunny summer, but with everything else going so well in the right direction, the weather didn't matter. Now that Rana was unwell, the darkness began to descend on me too. Considering that Rana and I had met less than seven months ago, we had this strong symbiotic bond, which is normally only seen between twins and very close family members. Although we were not related by blood, everyone recognised us as mother and daughter.

There was no skipping along the path and no climbing up trees. We walked slowly into the woods, then stood by the pond, almost reverently gazing into the water. We wanted to be quiet, as not to disturb the animals that had gone into hibernation. I saw my own shadowy reflection in the water – only my own!

"Rana?" The girl had been standing by my side, then suddenly within an instant she wasn't there. She had made no sound as she disappeared. The dim sun had gone behind clouds and it was rapidly getting dark. I had no wish to be here in the dark, in fear of not finding my way home. But I had to find Rana! I walked all around the pond, calling her name. When I reached the footpath, there was a rustling behind me.

"Rana?" I turned around to see a man walking towards me. I quickened my pace and heard laughter behind me. I ran. I arrived home at sunset.

When there was still no trace of Rana the following day, I walked with my dog up to the police station and reported her missing. Although many locals had met

Rana and had only good words to say about her, she was not officially registered anywhere. She was on no electoral roll and seemed to have no papers to identify herself. No passport, no bank account, no phone, no email, nothing. The police found nothing on or off line from the photograph, name or date of birth. She had organised business deals, ads and transactions, but took no credit for anything – all was done in my name. Rumours spread fast, that she had made up that name and possibly her date of birth, too. She had a fascination for frogs and picked a name in line with that. Rana means Frog in Greek or Latin and Marsh of course, is where a frog might live. Still this was hard to make sense of. A crook or a criminal would have deceived others in that way, but not Rana.

"She has done nothing bad. On the contrary, no one has ever helped me as much in my whole life. If it weren't for her, I would still be on the dole scrimping around. She has marketed my art work and within weeks established a thriving business, with money left to give to charity. We had so many orders recently, that we had to turn some away. She did everything, including all the financial stuff, which I'm hopeless at. She could do absolutely everything, like magic!" A detective came to my house and took the accounts book, as well as some of her drawings for examination. He picked a hair off one of Rana's dresses she had made and said he would hand it to forensics for DNA analysis.

Life carried on. I was alone in the house again, except for my cat and dog. I missed sharing my home, dinners, conversations, chores, fun and laughter. But life carried on, and thankfully, my business carried on, too and continued to grow.

Sharon phoned me:

"I have great news! I'm so excited! Melanie, my daughter, is getting married! So, next May I'm going to Australia for the wedding. I'm so happy, although she's probably invited her Dad as well, but we don't have to sit together."

"Congratulations!" I said flatly, unable to hide my disappointment that my friend's good news was not to do with Rana.

"Will you help me shop for my outfit? And make me a hat?"

"Yes, sure." I agreed.

Halloween came along. At first I was not in the mood to dress up and go out, but we had made everyone's costumes and it would be a pity not to wear them now. Between us, Rana and I had made Halloween costumes for ourselves and for Sharon and Elaine. As usual Rana had done most of the sewing and all the measuring. She only needed to look at my friends to guess their sizes and set to work with scissors and sewing machine, and in just a few hours everything fitted perfectly. Rana would have worn her favourite colour, green and my outfit was a different shade of green. Sharon was in purple and Elaine in blue. So the three wise fairy godmothers took their wands and walked up to the club, determined to have an enjoyable night out. Everyone who had made an effort to dress up was given a drink on the house. The music was great, so we spent a lot of time on the dance floor making the free drinks last a good while. It all helped to take my mind off the heartbreak of losing Rana. Frankenstein joined us, with some sort of alien reptile that kept stumbling over its long scaly tail. Some of the costumes were brilliant. I took a lot of photos. Sharon even made a short video of me dancing with Frankenstein and Elaine with the reptile.

"You know who that is?" Sharon whispered in my ear. "The t-rex, or whatever he is trying to be, is Elaine's ex-husband." I looked at the reptile still dancing although one of his scaly legs had dropped off, then at the video on Sharon's phone, and burst out laughing for the first time in three weeks.

"Does she know?" I asked. Sharon nodded vigorously, then laughed seeing his other leg fall off as he tripped over his tail and fell to the floor.

"The inebriated newt," I remembered.

"Or the legless lizard!" Now we could hardly control ourselves. Elaine pulled him up and tried to help him reassemble his scaly bits. Frankenstein laughed out loud. Where have I heard that laugh before? I did not recognise the man behind the monster paint, but his voice was familiar.

"Not the most comfortable costume," he said about the reptile, "yours are beautiful. Did you make them yourselves?"

"I helped making them," I said, "my very talented young lodger made them."

"The girl that went missing?" I stared at him.

"I saw you in the woods looking for her," he explained, "I was going to help you, but you ran away from me."

"Sorry, I..."

"No problem," he shrugged his huge Frankenstein shoulders. "Would you like another drink?" I accepted. He went to the bar. Elaine sat in a cosy corner with her ex, looking like she was too pleased to see him again. She later told me that he had given up the drink and they were happy to give their marriage another try, after fifteen years of separation. Lots of luck to them!

My phone buzzed. I went outside to answer. It was the police, only to tell me that they still had not found Rana and the case had totally puzzled them.

"We found no finger prints on any of the items examined," said the detective, "and even more peculiar, the results returned from the forensic lab as 'no human dna found – unknown species.'"

Frankenstein returned with two cocktails.

"Are you o.k.? Not bad news, I hope." Buried under his monster make-up was a genuine decent and attractive man, that I could trust completely. So I repeated to him what the detective had just told me. He shrugged his wide shoulders again.

"That's a bit weird alright." So we chatted, danced and chatted and danced. He liked the same freestyle dances that I did, and when a slow tune came on we sat down and finished our cocktails. By the end of the night we found we had a lot in common. He even knew about the pond and said he would try to help me find Rana. We would meet up again. He typed my number into his phone and rang it, so I would have his.

"My name is Adam," he said, smiling through his monster make up. "Adam Riley."

23

Tickets for the Concert

Tickets for the Concert

The night of the concert finally arrived. Rebecca had been notching up the days on the calendar, since we had queued up a whole day in the freezing cold to get tickets.

Now her excitement was catching like a bug. Never mind homework, hair extensions were more important right now.

I was running around like the proverbial fly to make sure of all the practical things like the tickets.

"Oh my God, where did I put those tickets?" In the jewellery box? No. The cutlery tray? Whenever I couldn't find something I would look in the most impossible places. We still had an hour to get everything ready. My husband wasn't coming, but he would have to drive us there and pick us up again.

"You're gonna need earplugs," he'd said.

"Oh, they're not that bad. I quite like some of their songs."

"You won't hear much of the music with all those screaming kids," he insisted. He had been young and fun to be with once himself. Now, he was moody and often impatient. I was still young at heart.

"Where are those wretched tickets?" I rummaged through the sock drawers and pulled out things like stockings and underwear I didn't know I had. Surely, I hadn't kept those things for Rebecca.

These look like new and they're not my size.

"What do you think, Mum?" Rebecca came in

with her hair extensions.

"You look lovely." She held up her hand with two tickets and I sighed with relief. I was going to deal with those purple knickers later!

24

Whiskey and Tears

Whiskey and Tears

Train trips were frequent a couple of decades ago. I lived in Dorset and worked at art and craft fairs in Cornwall the occasional weekend. I sat on the train for long hours and a good book usually helped. However, interesting people passed the time faster. There was always someone to chat to at some point. Teenagers playing card games, older people with friendly dogs. Once an old man brought his pet rat called Jezebel. He hid bits of cheese in his multiple pockets and the little animal ran up and down his arm looking for it, and eventually always found the food. She sat on his shoulder scrutinising the passengers – some laughed and some cringed. I was the only one who allowed Jezebel to run up my arm, across my back, down the other arm, back into the man's big coat pocket. She went to sleep in that pocket once she had enough cheese.

One day on a return trip I took with me the unpleasant souvenir of a broken heart and tried hard not to cry into my coffee. The couple opposite were more cheerful, then - well, they were a couple!

"Do you want some whiskey?" the woman asked me.

"No thanks," I replied.

"Ah go on, it'll cheer you up." So I allowed her to pour some whiskey into my coffee. What harm could it do? A few minutes later she knew all about me and the events of the last few days. Alcohol loosens the tongue. The woman told me she had been in much the same situation not long ago.

"We've all been there, not the end of the world." She was calm, though tipsy. She put her arm around her man, who sat next to her quietly drinking. He didn't say much, but looked happy. In another few minutes I was well cheered up. When the couple staggered off the train, we all wished each other "Good Luck!" I never saw them again. I couldn't get back into my book, dozed off to pleasant dreams and nearly missed my stop. Life was going in the right direction, like the train.

Acknowledgements

Acknowledgements

A million thanks to Kilkenny Writers Group at Loughboy Library, for keeping me writing with enthusiasm every Thursday afternoon. Many stories started there and were brought to life by the encouragement of the members of the group. I couldn't thank you enough, also for the discipline of getting me to sit down and write every week, something I would not be able to do at home. Special thanks to Doris Long for introducing me to the group, and the staff of Loughboy Library.

Many thanks to Ken Bourke, whose writing workshops inspired some of the stories in this book.

Special thanks to Gabriel Murray, at Dun Emer Press, for publishing this book.

Dun Emer Press.
2016

Printed in Great Britain
by Amazon